Loving Christ Through Time In Rhyme

Margaret Story

PublishAmerica
Baltimore

© 2012 by Margaret Story.
All rights reserved. No part of this book may be reproduced, stored in a retrieval system or transmitted in any form or by any means without the prior written permission of the publishers, except by a reviewer who may quote brief passages in a review to be printed in a newspaper, magazine or journal.

First printing

PublishAmerica has allowed this work to remain exactly as the author intended, verbatim, without editorial input.

Softcover 9781462662234
PUBLISHED BY PUBLISHAMERICA, LLLP
www.publishamerica.com
Baltimore

Printed in the United States of America

Dedication:

To my wonderful family: Nicki, my daughter, Chad, my son-in law, my wonderful grandsons: Tyler and Austin. Also to my son, Jon, who did some of the artwork for me. I am so blessed to have each one of you in my life . You all give me tremendous joy and purpose in my life, and I am very proud of each one of you.

Also to The Sunshine Sisters. How grateful I am for our group: Merty (Myra), Gerty (Gail), and Flerty (Linda) Sunshine. Also, our "fill-ins": Berty (Angie), Derty (Cheryl), and Perty (Lynne) Sunshine. You bring so much more than just joy and laughter to my heart.

To my sister-in-law, Tanger, You show me how to be strong, courageous and loving in the way you live your own life. Thanks for your inspiration.

Last but not least, of course, my husband Randy. You are the love of my life and I don't know how you put up with all of my shenanigans, but I am certainly grateful that you do. Thank you always, for the uncountable joys you bring to my life, and for all of the little things you have done to help me in this endeavor.

To all of you, as well as the many others who make my life so worthwhile, I give you my most sincere gratitude for the love and encouragement you all give to me every single day.

...After Jesus said these things, He looked toward heaven and prayed, "Father, the time has come. Give glory to Your Son so that the Son can give glory to You. . You gave the Son power over all people so that the Son could give eternal life to all those You gave Him. And this is eternal life: that people know You, the only true God, and that they know Jesus Christ, the One You sent. Having finished the work You gave Me to do, I brought You glory on earth. And now, Father, give Me glory with You; give Me the glory I had with You before the world was made...John 17: 1 – 5 NCV...Make them ready for Your service through Your truth; Your teaching is truth. I have sent them into the world, just as You sent Me into the world. ...I pray for these followers, but I am also praying for those who will believe in Me because of their teaching. Father I pray that they can be one. As You are in me and I am in You, I pray that they also can be one in Us...I will be in them and You will be in Me so that they will be completely one. Then the world will know that You sent Me and that You loved them just as much as You loved me. Father I want these people that You gave Me to be with Me where I am. I want them to see My glory, which You gave me because You loved Me before the world was made...I showed them what You are like, and I will show them again. Then they will have the same love that You have for Me, and I will live in them."

   ...John 17: 17, 18, 20, 21, 23, 24, & 26 NCV

From The Author:

This is a book of poetry on the life of Jesus Christ. I have tried to keep as close to Biblical truth as possible, but please remember that the poetry itself is a work of fiction. I believe with all of my heart that the Holy Bible was written through the inspiration of God's Holy Spirit being breathed into man. It is complete in its entirety. It cannot be added to or taken away from. It is God's holy, living, and breathing word; just as relevant yesterday, today, and tomorrow…in other words, true for all of time.

I do not believe God's Holy Spirit has breathed upon me as He did the apostles of His time. That was a holy inspiration breathed only into His chosen ones, that they might make a permanent, record for man, from God, of His Holy Word. I do believe however, that God **still** inspires people today, in many minute ways, for He is our God for all of time, not just of the past. Webster's New World Dictionary , Third College Edition defined inspiration this way:

inspiration: 1) a breathing in, as of air into the lungs; inhaling…2) an inspiring, or being inspired mentally or emotionally…3a) an inspiring influence; any stimulus to creative thought or action…3b) an inspired idea or action, etc.…4) a prompting of something to be written or said…5) Theological: a divine influence upon human beings, as that resulting in the writing of the Scriptures

I would never claim to have received His divine influence as did the writers of God's holy word – 1) and 5), but I do claim 2), 3), and 4). My poetry will not change the world, but perhaps, a line, a verse, a poem, or maybe the book itself, just might cause someone to stop and ponder on God, and His everlasting love for man-kind. Perhaps someone might even pick up the Bible to do a little research. **How wonderful that would be!** It is my sincere hope and prayer that this might happen. This is the whole purpose of my book. If some words or phrases seem repetitious, it is because I feel they need to be! The

Bible repeats phrases and lessons all of the time. If I repeat an idea, it is because I believe it cannot be said too often! It is too important to just say once! Words like receive, believe, cost, loss, faith, sacrifice and love. Words like these are such an integral part of the messages of the gospel.

KJV is my go to, and memory verse Bible. However, other versions can be easier to understand. Not paraphrased – that is not the same as Bible versions. There is a difference between paraphrasing and Bible versions. I have learned much from comparing other versions, and studying them all together with the KJV. If someone takes the time to study and compare different versions, along with the KJV, they are bound to draw closer to God. That alone will reap many great rewards! Try it! You won't like it, you'll come to LOVE it!

Before He was arrested, centuries before you and I were even born, Jesus prayed for all of you in the Garden of Gethsemane. I pray for you too, because I believe this is what He would have all of us to do: to lift one another up in prayer and supplication. I will pray without ceasing, as Jesus told us to do, for all of the souls lost to His will, and for those working to spread His truth.

He tells us to be silent and listen for His still, small voice. Have you listened for Him lately? He listens to each of us, anytime we call on Him. Will you not call on Him today…maybe to repent, maybe to ask for mercy or maybe…just to say "Thank You", or "I love You?" I know He would love to hear from you…even if you whisper.

With this in mind, I would like to thank my Lord Jesus Christ for all of the people, words and love He sends to me for my own brand of "inspiration". I couldn't write anything without His whisper in my heart, and I wouldn't last a day without His presence in my life.

I would also like to acknowledge with grateful appreciation all of the help from PublishAmerica in this, the printing of my first book. To all of you, "Blessed be."

Table of Contents

A Prayer of Hope For You 10
Who Was This Man Called Jesus? 12
A Pledge For His Believers 14
A Believer's Affirmation of Christ's Birth 16
The Holy Spirit Quells An Old Man's Doubt 18
Two Mothers Who Believed 20
The Chosen Father Who Believed 24
Night of Wonders 26
Two Temple Believers 30
King Above All Kings 32
Early Prophesies Fulfilled 36
The Faithful Nazarene 38
The Baptism of Jesus Christ 40
Temptations In The Wilderness 42
For Christ This Life Is Chosen 44
Water Into Wine 48
Son Of Man, Light of the World, King Upon God's Throne 50
What News This? 54
The Ministry of Christ 58
Jesus Speaks of Love 60
Love Reaches Across All Boundaries 64
The Faith of The Centurion 66
When Two Miracles Converged 68
What Are You Among So Many? 70
Take A Walk On Water 72
What Yeast This? 76
Who Will Enter The Heavenly Kingdom? 80
What Jesus Knew 84
Making Preparations 88
Something To Talk About: The Hearts of The Pharisees 92
The Lord's Last Supper 94
Betrayal's Cost 96

Prediction's Truth, Denial's Cost	100
Jesus Stood On Trial	104
Behold The Cross	108
What Price Glory?	112
Paying Tribute	116
Joy Comes In The Morning	118
O Ye Of Little Faith	120
On Faith Alone	124
Appearance By The Sea	128
Revelation's Promise	130
A Trust To Keep Have I	134
My Father's Love	136
In The Circle Of Jesus' Love	138
Why Won't You Come?	140
The Family of God	144
A Prayer of Need	146
God's Answer To A Prayer of Need	148
How Many Times Must Ye Be Told?	150
Christ, The Greatest Miracle Of All	154

...Moreover as for me, God forbid that I should sin against the Lord in ceasing to pray for you: but I will teach you the good and the right way: Only fear the Lord, and serve Him in truth with all your heart; for consider how great things He hath done for you...
I Samuel 12: 23 & 24 KJV...I am coming to You now, but I say these things while I am still in the world, so that they may have the full measure of My joy within them...Sanctify them by the truth; Your word is truth. As You sent Me into the world, I have sent them into the world. My prayer is not for them alone. I pray also for those who will believe in Me through their message, that all of them may be one, so that the world may believe that You have sent Me. I in them and You in Me. May they be brought to complete unity to let the world know that You sent me and have loved them even as You have loved Me...
John 13: 10, 13, 17, 18, 20 & 21 NIV

A Prayer of Hope For You

This prayer of hope I send to you all
that you too may hear the Master's call.
While I pray for those who love our Lord,
I pray most for those who pay Him no accord.

I believe His love should be passed along,
not to be left barren upon a worldly throne.
Your life is yours to live as you choose,
but in not choosing Him, I believe you lose.
You may want to live as you see fit,
but in loving Christ, you don't lose a bit.
You gain more than any could truly know.
Why not give Him the chance His love to show?

There are more who doubt, than who dare to believe.
Who will not give Him a glance, or His word receive.
Yet would not more joy, peace, love and strength,
be worth any price, make you go any length?

Would not more power than you can hold in your hand,
be greater than any treasure throughout the whole land?
You can even be victorious when you face defeat,
with His grace in you, your trials to meet.

Instead of fighting life's battles alone,
why not grab hold the anchor both loving and strong?
Why not reach for more than this world can give?
Why not reach for eternity with the Savior to live?

Life can be full, you think, "I'll catch Him later;
but if tomorrow doesn't come, then which would be greater?
To face your life's end, wondering where will I go?
Or to meet with a Savior and His Paradise to know?

The choice is quite simple, but it is yours to make.
How I pray for those lost or too busy to take
the time to seek His love, so much greater than you know.
Please give Him a chance, and watch your life grow.

If you just ask Him in, He will most gladly come
and bring you a new life that at once is begun.
He will open new doors you would never have seen
and give you more joy than any other could bring.

To believe, or to not, the choice: yours alone.
Will you seek out His love for your very own?
You have only to choose, what path will you take?
I pray you choose His, your life richer to make.

And I hope and pray too, that these writings I give
will help bring you some joy, peace and love as you live.
And I pray that His love will lead you to your place
where He can be found, with His love and grace.
Amen

...In the beginning was the Word, and the Word was with God, and the Word was God. He was with God in the beginning. Through Him all things were made; without Him nothing was made that has been made. In Him was life, and that life was the Light of men. The Light shines in the darkness, but the darkness has not understood it...He was in the world, and though the world was made through Him, the world did not recognize Him. He came to that which was His own, but His own did not receive Him. Yet to all who received Him, to those who believed in His name, He gave the right to become children of God – children born not of natural descent, nor of human decision or a husband's will, but born of God. The Word became flesh and made His dwelling among us. We have seen His glory, the glory of the One and Only, who came from the Father, full of grace and truth....John 1: 1 – 5, 10 – 14 NIV...He shall be great, and shall be called the Son of the Highest;...and He shall reign over the house of Jacob forever; and of His kingdom there shall be no end...Luke 1: 3 & 33 KJV...

Who Was This Man Called Jesus?

Who was this man called Jesus? Why was He sacrificed?
The son of man, the Son of God? Why paid He such a price?
Why did God send a Savior, with ways above the rest?
It's clear He stood above all trials, passed with faith, each human test.
Here was a man of goodness, no other has surpassed.
His love for man so powerful, forever it will last.

No one from God be turned away, the Word brought God to us all.
People still listen everywhere, believers still send out His call.
All He ever asked of us: to live as we were bidden.
As if a child, believe in Him, let not our love be hidden.
Our hearts are not to overflow with pretense, show and tell.
Our hearts are to be humble, and our love to grow and swell.
Jesus brought God's message, to all who would believe.
We just have to listen, trust in our faith, and then receive.
We must pass along His message, just as the Father so desires.

Ignite in others that we meet, a spark to light their fires.
Who was this man called Jesus…just the Savior of the world.
Come join with His believers, let His message be unfurled!
Tell all this man called Jesus is the Son of God Most High.
He came to bring God's love to all, let us bring His children nigh.
Throw out the lifeline of God's love, the way our Savior did.
Keep His light shining ever bright, let not Hid love be hid.
Who was this man called Jesus? Search the scriptures, you will find
the message that can give each life true joy and peace of mind.

...Blessed is every one that feareth the Lord; that walketh in His ways. For thou shalt eat the labour of thine hands: happy shalt thou be, and it shall be well with thee...
   Psalm 128: 1 & 2 KJV

A Pledge For His Believers

Heavenly Father, to Thee above
we pledge our hearts this day in love.
As we build upon our lives each day,
may we build on our faith in the same way.

May we draw each hour, ever closer to Thee,
and live daily our faith for everyone to see.
Not just with words by our faith to stand,
but by all our deeds among our fellowman.

May we build upon all that Jesus has taught,
and walk in His steps as we know that we ought.
May we strive each day for His love and His peace,
working together for all hatred to cease.

May we search for justice, help good will to grow,
sharing Thy mercies with all here below.
Let us be Your beacon, for all the world to see.
May we stay ever loyal and faithful, to Thee.

A better path than His, we know we can't find.
Bring us His heart and enlighten each mind.
Help us to share with all others we meet,
the greatest joys of life come from Him, if we seek.

Mouth to mouth, heart to heart, giving all that we can,
helping others to find Him, divinity in man.

"Go and tell," Jesus told us, this be our task:
to tell others of God's love is all Jesus would ask.

While yet so important, for many hard to hear.
Still we put forth the effort, for to us He's so dear.
We want to share Him, bring more to His fold,
Just as the prophets long ago have foretold.

Guide Father, our footsteps, pick us up when we falter.
Teach us Thy ways to bring more to Thy alter.
Christ is our King and our voices we raise
To bring Him the honor, the glory, and praise.

...And the Word was made flesh, and dwelt among us, (and we beheld His glory, the glory as of the only begotten of the Father,) full of grace and truth...John 1: 14 KJV

A Believer's Affirmation of Christ's Birth

We believe in God our Father, maker of heaven and earth,
and we believe in His gift of love passed down in Jesus' birth.
We believe a Holy Virgin brought forth her first-born son,
and we believe He is our King, a Savior for everyone.
We believe in the humble stable where the tiny babe was born,
and we believe in the angel's chorus and their guarded watch 'til morn.
We believe that shepherds came to see this wondrous sight,
and we believe the wise men came, guided by a star day bright.
We believe God's special gift was of greatest sacrifice,
and we believe salvation's promise can only come through Christ.
We believe the joys of Christ can fill our lives with song,
and we believe our love for Him should shine bright all year long.
We believe that peace on earth, good will should ever ring,
and we give thanks with all our hearts, for the babe that would be King.

...But the angel said unto him, "Fear not Zacharias: for thy prayer is heard; and thy wife Elizabeth shall bear thee a son, and thou shalt call his name John. And thou shalt have joy and gladness; and many shall rejoice at his birth. For he shall be great in the sight of the Lord, and shall drink neither wine nor strong drink; and he shall be filled with the Holy Ghost, even from his mother's womb. And many of the children of Israel shall he turn to the Lord their God."...Luke 1: 13 - 16 KJV

The Holy Spirit Quells An Old Man's Doubt

Elizabeth and Zacharias longed for a child to call their own,
but old age had crept upon them, it appeared the chance was gone.
While praying in the temple, Zacharias heard God's angel say,
"Fear not your prayer's been answered, you soon shall have your way.
The womb of your wife shall be filled with the Holy Ghost, and lo,
the child that you have longed for, then you will come to know.
His name you shalt call John, he'll be great in the Father's sight.
He shall proclaim the coming of God's only Chosen Light.
You both shall know great joy, and many others will rejoice.
John shall go forth in God's Spirit, and declare in a loud voice:
for all to come unto God's Shepherd, to repent their sinful fall.
That Christ soon would stand among them, His fallen lambs to call.
Your son shall be God's messenger, sent to prepare Messiah's way."
But Zacharias doubted what God's angel had come to him to say.
He dared to answer back that such old age could not conceive.
The angel Gabriel answered, "Because my words you don't believe,
for this you will be silenced until John's birth is done."
Thus Zacharias could not speak 'til the day he named his son.
When John was brought into the temple on his day of circumcision,
Zacharias named the child as was his God's decision.
He knew now that his son would be prophet of the Most High.
He would lay the groundwork needed, the Messiah's time was nigh.
Zacharias raised his praise, for his doubt had now been quelled.

In gratitude, he did rejoice, in God's spirit he too dwelled.
The Holy Spirit always faithful, fulfilled now, the Father's call.
Over Israel, and all other lands, evil soon would start to fall.

...When Elizabeth heard Mary's greeting, the baby leaped in her womb, and Elizabeth was filled with the Holy Spirit. In a loud voice she exclaimed: "Blessed are you among women, and blessed is the child you will bear!...Blessed is she who has believed that what the Lord has said to her will be accomplished!"...Luke 1: 41, 42 & 45 NIV

Two Mothers Who Believed

Mary was a young girl when the Lord's angel came to call.
A virgin espoused to Joseph, who knew and lived God's holy law.
The news the angel told her, how she would give birth to a son,
to her, seemed so unlikely; her life as wife had not begun.
Yet the angel after calming her, explained her virgin birth.
How God's Spirit soon would fill her with a womb of greatest worth.
For Mary had found favor with the Lord; she'd soon conceive
the child so long awaited, as the prophets had believed.

With God all things are possible, this Mary firmly did believe.
If this was to be the Lord's will, she was ready to receive.
She'd do what 'ere God bid her, she would face all those who'd doubt.
Being united with God's Spirit, was what her life was all about.
She only prayed the husband to whom she soon was to be wed,
would accept this holy child and all the things that Gabriel said.
She would not fret or worry, for God's will would be done.
She just needed to be patient, await the birth of her first son.

Then too, Gabriel told her of another birth proclaimed,
to her barren, elder cousin; this too a miracle yet not the same.
She traveled far to see Elizabeth, her cousin, held so dear.
The babe inside Elizabeth leaped in joy as Mary neared.
When Elizabeth saw her cousin, with God's Spirit in her voice,
she gave to Mary greeting while rejoicing in God's choice.
"Blessed are you among women, and blessed is your child;
blessed are you for believing in this miracle meek and mild.

In my womb my child did leap, with joy and anticipation
for the birth of you dear Son, who will come to save our nation."
"My soul doth magnify the Lord," Mary's answer was begun.
"That He would use His humble handmaid to deliver such a Son.
All generations will call me blessed, that this He's done for me.
I will praise my Lord, the Mighty One, for His mercy I can see.
Through this child mercy will come for all who fear His name.
The proud ones will be brought down by the power He has claimed.

The rulers of all kingdoms who reject this chosen Son
will fall in ruin and chaos once His final time has come.
Yet, the humble, they will praise Him, for the mercies they'll receive.
For He has come to save them, if in Him they will believe.
He feeds the hungry with good things, selfish rich He'll turn away.
His Son will rule forever, just as the prophets once did say."
When Mary left her cousin to return to her own home,
she knew the task she now faced would be hard to face alone.

She did not know at first just how her Joseph would react,
it might not be his will to marry, since her condition was intact.
But still she faced with courage, what she knew was meant to be,
and public humiliation would not change her one degree.
Even though she knew the customs, if unwed girls conceived,
she was willing to be undaunted as God's Spirit she received.
God's will was most important, she prayed Joseph would understand,
and that he too would not falter, but would choose by God to stand.

This babe she bore within her was to be God's holy will.
In her heart she knew the Lord's plans always were fulfilled.
Only time would tell if she and Joseph would be wed.
Still in her heart she did believe all Gabriel had said.
To God she would be faithful, no matter what the cost.
To do God's will as bidden, she never counted as a loss.
The handmaid of the Most High, in much wonder and awe
marched bravely forward to the beat of destiny's new call.

Her thoughts she kept unto herself, awaiting, faithful, true.
Praying that Joseph too would see the things that he must do.
She would wait most patient, in spite of talk spinning around.
She had new purpose in her heart, her faith to God was bound.
Many would doubt and wonder, would think she was to blame.
She knew she had done nothing to bring about such shame.
Daily praying, watching, her life was changed forevermore.
The world would change forever too, once she gave birth unto its Lord.

...Then Joseph being raised from sleep did as he angel of the Lord had bidden him, and took unto him his wife: And knew her not till she had bought forth her firstborn son: and he called his name Jesus... Matthew 1: 24 & 25 KJV

The Chosen Father Who Believed

While Mary waited for the decision, her espoused husband soon must make,
Joseph being a just, devout man, wondered what path he should take.
His righteousness would not let him wish for her public disgrace.
Should he divorce her quietly, send her to some other place?
While pondering on the matter, in sleep, God's angel came
and told him to not be afraid, for Mary bore no shame.

Gabriel told him of the virgin birth that Mary soon would bear.
How through them as parents, new life man-kind soon could share.
Believing in God's Spirit, Joseph now felt there was no strife.
Thus, he took Mary, his beloved, to be his wedded wife.
Still he touched her not, the marriage union was not done.
He knew that now, he had no doubt, this would be God's own Son.

Now all of this was done that the scripture's be fulfilled:
"Behold a virgin's Son who would be called "Emanuel".
As instructed Joseph named the child, Jesus, at His birth.
For His name would be the holiest of any name on earth.
The child Mary delivered, came from the Lord Most High.
Oh, how they both adored Him, as by the laws they did abide.

They took Him as a baby to Jerusalem's temple square,
to make the accustomed sacrifice that all their people shared.
To be purified by circumcision, as all firstborn males must be,
for since the Law of Moses this had been the Jew's decree.
Perhaps Joseph remembered that when man-kind fell to sin,
Jehovah promised them a Savior, man-kind's victory to win.

Even though His children failed Him, God vowed not do the same.
He would give to all His mercy, through His Chosen One's sweet name.
It would cost Him greatest sacrifice, but His Spirit He would send,
to give to all His children, again the chance to call God friend.
We may not know the thoughts this chosen earthly father felt,
but we know that he stayed true in heart, when with him God had dwelt.

...And so it was, that, while they were there, the days were accomplished that she should be delivered. And she brought forth her firstborn son, and wrapped Him in swaddling clothes, and laid Him in a manger; because there was no room for them in the inn. And there were in the same country shepherds abiding in the field, keeping watch over their flock by night. And, lo, the angel of the Lord came upon them, and the glory of them: and they were sore afraid... And it came to pass, as the angels were gone away from them into heaven, the shepherds said one to another, "Let us now go even unto Bethlehem, and see this thing which is come to pass, which the Lord hath made known unto us."...And when they had seen it, they made known abroad the saying which was told them concerning this child...
    Luke 2: 6, 7 - 9, 15, 16 & 17 KJV

Night of Wonders

In darkest night, in a busy little town,
travelers hustled and bustled all around.
Every inn in town was full that night,
packed to the streets, packed close and tight.
No room could be found, not one anywhere.
Only darkness and noise were left there to share.

Came a tired, young couple, seeking some rest.
She was with child, he was trying his best;
to find her some shelter but none could be found,
even though he'd searched through all Bethlehem town.
Worried, Joseph begged of the last innkeeper,
"She'll deliver soon! Somewhere I must keep her!"

The innkeeper was weary of travelers galore.
Still he saw the deep burden that Joseph bore.
Stepping across people lying in the streets,
he motioned to Joseph to be most discreet.
"I'll tell you where you might find some rest,
but don't tell the others, for I must confess:

It's just a stable, in the back, and it's bare.
It hasn't much light or any warmth to share.
It's a fitting place for cows and sheep.
But not such as a newborn babe should sleep.
Still, if with the animals you will share,
then I will be willing to lead you there."

So to a humble and dark abode,
an expectant, virgin mother rode.
Upon a donkey, small yet sweet,
led by husband Joseph, so weary and beat.
He made her a bed in soft, clean hay,
and found a manger where the babe could lay.

Just before the dawn of morn's first light,
she gave birth to a boy of special might.
He'd come to save all of our sons and daughters.
In this stable bare, all history would be altered.
For this very child was the Father's own Son!
Through Him sin's dread sway would become undone.

In the country, as shepherds watched their flock;
they suddenly received a brilliant shock!
The heavens were filled with a holy light,
as an angel told them of Christ's birth that night.
How joy would soon spread throughout the land.
David's foretold Savior had come to man.

Then a host of angels joined in jubilee
of the baby sleeping at Mary's knee.
Wrapped in cloths, in a manger stall,
this child would bring joy and peace to all.
The shepherds left with haste to behold
the wonder of which the angels had told.

When they left that stable, no longer bare,
oh what a story they now had to share!
Amazed by the wonders they all had seen,
and how angels had sung of the newborn King.
Their tales spread quickly of this special birth,
as a brilliant star shone down to earth.

O night of wonders, so bold, so bright;
gladly we give homage for Thy gift of light.
For the life that began for us all anew,
as our Savior was born to give us His due.
O night of wonders, we will pass on along
the story of that night and it's love so strong.

All believers' hearts will forever ring
with love and praise for this child, our King.
Through all the centuries, 'til He comes once again
to reclaim His Kingdom before all of man.
He will rule all kingdoms, both heaven and earth.
This was His due from creation's first birth.

...When the time of their purification according to the Law of Moses had been completed, Joseph and Mary took Him to Jerusalem to present Him to the Lord (as is written in the Law of the Lord, "Every firstborn male is to be consecrated to the Lord")...Now there was a man in Jerusalem called Simeon, who was righteous and devout. He was waiting for the consolation of Israel, and the Holy Spirit was upon him...There was also a prophetess, Anna, the daughter of Phanuel, of the tribe of Asher...She never left the temple but worshipped night and day, fasting and praying...
Luke 2: 22, 23, 25, 36, & 37 NIV

Two Temple Believers

There was in the temple, a man just and much devout.
He had prayed he would not see death, till the day had come about
when he could see the new Messiah; and his prayer came true one day.
Christ was brought into the temple, and this Simeon had to say:
"Oh Lord, as you have promised, please let your servant leave in peace,
for my eyes see your salvation, now, my soul you can release."
To the couple he gave blessing, but warned Mary of the sword
that one day would pierce deep her heart, at the suffering of their Lord.

"Not just her heart, but Simeon's too, for the sacrifice to be made,
and yet the whole world would be changed, by this one tiny babe.
"The thoughts and hearts of many would one day be revealed,
through the pain that they must suffer when His destiny was fulfilled."
Day and night there in the temple, was a widow who always stayed,
and constantly she fasted, served the Lord, and too, she prayed.
Immediately upon seeing the child that the parents brought,
she too gave her blessings, and they pondered all these thoughts.

Then the family left for Galilee, to a town called Nazareth.
The prophecies now had come true, yet much to do was left.
Jesus would be raised in a home filled with God's love,

and He would be taught how He came from God above.
Still even without teaching, Jesus knew His Father's will,
for through the Holy Spirit, too soon all would be fulfilled.
Here grew the child that one day, would be man-kind's saving grace.
Into the heart of Jesus, the Father's love, the Spirit placed.

No other love is stronger than is the love of just these Three.
The Father, Son and Holy Ghost, are as one in harmony.
Three separate identities, in one spirit they are the same.
And only through the Son of God, can the Holy Ghost be claimed.
One is not without the other, belief must be in all the Three.
Every knee will bow, all tongues confess, throughout eternity,
that God the Father, Christ the Son, the Holy Spirit, all as one,
is the Alpha and Omega, and through one God the victory's won.

...The kings of the earth set themselves, and the rulers take counsel together, against the Lord and against His anointed, saying...Yet have I set My King upon My holy hill of Zion...Be wise now therefore, O ye kings: be instructed, ye judges of the earth. Serve the Lord with fear, and rejoice with trembling. Kiss the Son, lest He be angry, and ye perish from the way, when His wrath is kindled but a little. Blessed are they that put their trust in Him...Psalm 2: 2, 6, 10 – 12 KJV

King Above All Kings

Before Christ was taken to grow up in Nazareth town
a jealous king decided that none should take his crown.
The lands around all Bethlehem, had heard the shepherd's story.
But King Herod in his splendor, heard not of the baby's glory,
until the time that wise men came; three kings from foreign lands,
seeking to find the Christ child who would become the King of man.

They had been following the light of His brightly shining star.
In a caravan of camels, they had come from distance far.
They'd studied all the prophecies, the ones that had foretold
of a Savior to be born to all, a man both brave and bold.
The star still shone before them, but to reach their destination,
they asked King Herod if he'd help them find the right location.

They asked if he knew the city where this child was to be born?
But King Herod became jealous and in his heart grew only scorn.
He gave unto the wise men a deceptive, smiling face.
Told them they should let him know if they found His resting place.
Then he could go himself, bow down, and worship this King too.
But in his heart and mind he planned just what he'd really do.

After checking with his council, He sent the kings away,
to Bethlehem, where the prophets had foretold the child would lay.
The wise men left the palace, not knowing that the king
was even then deciding how he could halt this thing.

This child would someday try to take his kingdom from his hand?
Not as long as he ruled would this child be such a man!
.
The wise men saw again the star, still shining ever bright.
Once more they were guided by it's light both day and night.
Soon would be found this wonder that so diligently they sought.
They would honor and adore the child with offerings they had brought.
Signs had brought them to the star, the star brought them to the babe.
As it rested high above the place wherein the child now laid.

Gold, frankincense and myrrh, were the gifts they wished to share.
Such as would be so befitting such a royal King this rare.
Then being warned by dream of King Herod's dreaded plans,
the wise men quickly left and traveled home through other lands.
Furious with jealousy, King Herod made this wretched vow!
He'd have his soldiers find and destroy this King somehow!

He sent for his loyal soldiers with plans to kill this child,
but the Father's close protection, would not be defiled.
Herod's greatest plots would only meet with sad defeat,
for the Father had great purpose for His child so mild and sweet.
King Herod might try to destroy, and others would try too,
but God's promise of a Messiah could not be stopped from coming true.

The Father knew this child would be His greatest gift to man.
He knew the price He'd pay through Christ, to halt sin's strong demand.
There was much His Son would do when He came into His own.
And nothing anywhere could ever stop His love so strong.
God's children only need obey Him; believe in His child, foretold,
then He would bless each one of them with eternity's sweet fold.

This was the choice the God-head had long ago decided.
Before they started to create, before time was divided.

Before they spoke the words that formed the sky, the land, the sea.
Before the world that we now know had even come to be.
Before the great deceiver fell from God's most loving way.
Before the strong desires of man fell into evil's sway.

They knew a King would need to be the sacrificial Lamb,
to bring God's children back to Him, the Lord, the great I AM.
Then His beloved children, once more could live in peace,
in love and understanding; in joy that nevermore would cease.
To be one in the spirit, living forever with our King,
with singing and rejoicing for all eternity to ring!

...But you, Bethlehem Ephrathah, though you are small among the clans of Judah, out of you will come for Me one who will be ruler over Israel, whose origins are from of old, from ancient times...Micah 5: 2 NIV...After Jesus was born in Bethlehem in Judea, during the time of King Herod, Magi from the east came to Jerusalem and asked, "Where is the one who has been born King of the Jews? We saw His star in the east and have come to worship Him." When King Herod heard this he was disturbed, and all Jerusalem with him...And having been warned in a dream not to go back to Herod, they returned to their country by another route. When they had gone, an angel of the Lord appeared to Joseph in a dream. "Get up," he said, "take the child and his mother and escape to Egypt. Stay there until I tell you, for Herod is going to search for the child to kill him."...And so was fulfilled what the Lord had said through the prophet: "Out of Egypt I called My Son."...When Herod realized that he had been outwitted by the Magi, he was furious, and he gave orders to kill all the boys in Bethlehem and its vicinity who were two years old and under...Then what was said through the prophet Jeremiah was fulfilled: A voice is heard in Ramah, weeping and great mourning, Rachel weeping for her children and refusing to be comforted, because they are no more....After Herod died, an angel of the Lord appeared in a dream to Joseph in Egypt and said, "Get up, take the child and his mother to the land of Israel, for those who were trying to take the child's life are dead."...and he went and lived in a town called Nazareth. So was fulfilled what was said through the prophets: "He will be called a Nazarene."

Matthew 2: 3, 12, 13, & 14 – 21 & 23 NIV

Early Prophesies Fulfilled

Several early prophesies foretold of a special baby's birth,
and keeping watch were angels, with heralded songs to earth.
Animals resting in their beds, watched with wondering gaze,
as a baby wrapped in cloths was in a manger placed.
Some shepherds came to see the sight, of which the angels told,
as did three kings from distant lands, this wonder to behold.

The kings had studied prophesies, had seen His star's formation.
They brought Him treasured gifts and bowed in humble adoration.
They knew this tiny baby would become the greatest King.
As Mary pondered upon the sight, joy in her heart did ring.

All would not rejoice His birth, as King Herod's hatred grew.
The wise men had betrayed him, for through a dream they knew,
that jealous rage ruled Herod's heart, as he vowed his crown to keep.
With cruel injustice, fear and pain, soon all the land would weep.
For King Herod to his soldiers would give an angry, heartless law:
"Each male child, from two years down, beneath the blade should fall!
Not one be spared, or they would pay; " in fear they did as bidden.
Terror ruled throughout the land; such woe could not be hidden.
Just as the prophets had foretold, from the wilderness was heard,
heartbreaking grief as Rachel cried at Herod's killing word.

Her babies now lay dying all through-out the land.
She could not be consoled because of evil's killing hand.
In a midnight's dream to Joseph, before the die was cast,
God warned him, "Flee to Egypt, until the danger's past.
The prophets had foretold this too, in time all would be seen.
"Out of Egypt have I called my Son; He'll be called the Nazarene."
In time, God called to Joseph, "It's safe, now Herod's dead."
The family moved to Nazareth, just as prophets once had said.
This Savior came as was foretold, man's destiny was changed.
For God's forgiveness of our sins had always been arranged.

Prophecies foretold it, though much here would come true,
the greatest prophecy of all: what Christ would come to do.
Far below His ivory towers, Jesus chose the path to take.
He laid divinity aside and all for man-kind's sake.
Our sins would be washed pure as the whitest winter snow,
if we would just confess them, and choose the Christ to know.
Though prophets foretold all of this, more still would yet come true.
Other prophesies would be fulfilled, when Christ received His due.
For every knee shall bow and every tongue confess Him Lord.
He will rule all of creation from His throne forevermore.

...When He was twelve years old they went to the feast as they always did....After three days they found Jesus sitting in the Temple with the teachers, listening to them and asking them questions. All who heard him were amazed at his understanding and answers...Luke 2: 42, 46 & 47...NIV...For I came down from heaven, not to do mine own will, but the will of Him that sent me...And this is the will of Him that sent me, that every one which seeth the Son, and believeth on Him, may have everlasting life: and I will raise him up at the last day...John 6: 38, 40 KJV

The Faithful Nazarene

Even as a young child, Jesus sought God's way,
as He waxed strong in spirit, growing every day.
Came the time of Passover, and so the trip was made
by Jesus and His family, they had homage to be paid.

When the family started home, young Jesus stayed behind,
to share with temple elders, the wonders of His mind.
His parents had no idea just where their son could be,
and frightened they continued to seek him earnestly.

At twelve years He began, a much brighter world to make.
He wondered at His parents fear; He knew what path to take.
And as He grew to manhood, He left to seek God's will,
even though He knew that in time He must be killed.

This dark world so filled with both love and with hate,
left Him little choice for there could be no mistake.
Only the very greatest of all God could sacrifice
would pay in full the cost of sin's most dreaded, killing price.

Thus He started on His path to save our sons and daughters,
and from His Father's will, His steps would never falter.
The road would not be easy, there would be much pain and strife.
Yet ever faithful He would stand, even though it meant His life.

He came not to condemn the world, but to offer those who'd strayed,
redemption and salvation, if God's commands would be obeyed.
He'd heal all manner of illness, perform miracles never seen.
Word quickly spread throughout the lands about this Nazarene.

From where came all the power for the good that He could do?
Or the wisdom He would speak to man; were the scriptures coming true?
Could good come out of Nazareth, a town of ill repute?
Could hearts be changed, lives turned around, there seemed little dispute.

The multitudes would come in throngs each time that it was heard:
Christ was near, they'd want to see and hear His every word.
To the scriptures, He'd be true, and faithful to His Father.
No matter how tired He might become, His brethren were no bother.

He'd never alter in His path, He would greet each heart sincere,
and offer to each one God's love and friendship ever near.
Though much still faced this Nazarene, He would answer every knock,
for into His heart the secrets of His Father's will were locked.

No greater love can man-kind know, than to give one's life for others.
No greater love can we give back then the love we give our brothers.
This Nazarene was faithful, though this was no easy task.
His love was meant for each of us, what more could we dare ask?

His life for ours, our life for Him, why is there any doubt?
It's what the Savior lived for, what His life was all about.
Search the scriptures, you will see, it is plainly written there.
No sacrifice too great for Him, His love He meant to share.

...John answered, saying unto them all, I indeed baptize you with water; but one mightier than I cometh, the latchet of whose shoes I am not worthy to unloose; He shall baptize you with the Holy Ghost and with fire:...Luke 3: 16 KJV...And immediately the Spirit driveth Him into the wilderness...Mark 1: 12 KJV...And He saith unto them, "Follow Me, and I will make you fishers of men."...Matthew 4:19 KJV

The Baptism of Jesus Christ

Came the call from the wilderness by Jordan's river shore:
"Repent! Repent! Make straight today, the pathway of our Lord.
For there is one among you, the prophets said would come.
He will cleanse our darkest sins, He is the Father's Son.
I am not worthy to unlatch His shoe, He's here, can't you see?
Lord, I baptize with water, why comest Thou to me?"

But Jesus knew His righteousness needed to be fulfilled,
so He would remain forever close to His Father's holy will.
The deed was done, and lo, from the heavens up above
descended God's Holy Spirit in the form of one sweet dove.
"This is my beloved Son, in whom I am well pleased."
Came the voice from heaven. Sin's hold would start to cease.

John watched as Jesus left him, and from Jordan's riverside,
Christ headed to the wilderness, with His Father to abide.
He needed now His solitude and fellowship with God.
Much would come upon His path before He left earth's sod.
Only in communion with His Father would He find,
the strength and courage needed, evil's sway to bind.

To fulfill His chosen destiny, forty days of prayer He sought.
Victory carried heavy cost, but the battle must be fought.
His love for the Father must remain steadfast and true.
Equaled only by His love for man, He knew what He must do.

He had so little time to teach His brethren of God's love.
Too soon He would leave this life, for His heavenly throne above.

He'd fast and pray both day and night, to become completely filled.
To be one with the Father and the Holy Spirit's will.
Son of God, Son of man, with just one goal to seek:
to bring back to the Father, the lost, forlorn and weak.
The Trinity of one mind and goal, would show for all of time,
the magnitude of the Father's love, no other so sublime.

...And Jesus being full of the Holy Ghost returned from Jordan, and was led by the Spirit into the wilderness, Being forty days, tempted of the devil. And in those days, He did eat nothing; and when they were ended, He afterward hungered...Luke 4: 1, 2 KJV...Then the devil leaveth Him, and, behold, angels came and ministered unto Him....
   Matthew 4: 11 KJV

Temptations In The Wilderness

For forty days and forty nights, Christ fasted and He prayed,
in spirit with His Father, gaining strength to meet sin's sway.
Thus Satan came and Jesus knew the devil now would try
to tempt Him from His Father, with wealth and twisted lies.
Here are the temptations Satan used against our Lord.
Deceitfully He laid the trap, these are the words both swore:

"If Thou be the Son of God, command bread from these stones."
To which the Savior answered, "Man lives not by bread alone,
but with the very words of God, to which your ears are dead."
"Then jump Ye from this temple, for Ye will not harm Thy head."
"Satan tempt ye not thy God, for I will never falter."
Came Satan then to offer all he could from evil's alter.

Showing all the kingdoms he would give as consolation,
and all that Jesus had to do? Bow down and worship Satan!
In anger Jesus answered, to His Father, He'd be true!
God's angels came to minister to Christ as was His due.
Time was short, His path was straight, from the wilderness He came
to complete His given task of bringing honor to God's name.

He would gather His disciples, twelve very special men.
From all walks of life they'd come, their lives with Him to spend.
He'd teach them all He could, show them how they ought to live.
Then they would spread the good news that Christ had come to give.
By foot they'd travel far and wide, to let God's truth be known.
By word of mouth through generations, how God's family has grown.

All believers are God's disciples, telling everyone they meet,
the Father's love is in our hearts, temptations to defeat.
Though we may sometimes stumble, through trickery and deceit,
God's love will still be strong enough the devil to defeat.
The great deceiver, to himself, will tell the strongest lies;
for God's will cannot be conquered, no matter how he tries.

...And Jesus said unto them, Come ye after me, and I will make you to become fishers of men...And they were astonished at His doctrine; for He taught them as one that had authority, and not as the scribes... Mark 1: 17, 22,...Go ye therefore, and teach all nations, baptizing them in the name of the Father, and of the Son, and of the Holy Ghost Teaching them to observe all things whatsoever I have commanded you: and, lo, I am with you Always, even unto the end of the world. Amen....Matthew 28: 19 & 20 KJV

For Christ This Life Is Chosen

When Jesus came out of the wilderness, so much needed to be done,
but first He'd choose disciples, to finish teaching He'd begun.
Simon, who is called Peter, and Andrew, Simon's brother;
James, the son of Zebedee, and John, who was James' brother.

Philip and Bartholomew, also Thomas the one who'd doubt.
Matthew, the tax collector, who Simon complained about.
James, son of Alphaeus, Thaddaeus, and Simon the Cananite,
and Judas Iscariot who would alas, betray Christ in the night.

These are the twelve Christ chose, all but one of them believed.
These are the first apostles, His inner circle to achieve.
God's children needed teaching, and the rest of the world too.
He wanted men who would stand strong in all they had to do.

He'd have three years to teach the men about His Father's way.
He knew they would be tempted, and at times by evil swayed.
To some, the twelve He chose, would cause arguable surprise.
They were not leaders men would pick, as seen by worldly eyes.

The eyes of Christ saw deeper, than the eyes of man could go.
Though some might doubt His choices, He knew what each would sow.
Each man had his strengths, but too, each man had his faults,
but once accepting who Christ was, they'd continue what He taught.

Christ would teach how man should live according to God's plans,
and not let Satan tempt them from the Father's loving hands.
He would teach how man's salvation, could only come through Him.
How Satan's lies and trickery had made their view of God so dim.

He would show them many miracles and sights they'd never seen,
such as healings of the body, and hopeless spirits to be redeemed.
He would raise the sick from dying, without even being present;
tell how God loved a faithful heart, whether from the rich or peasant.

He would teach of the new Kingdom, He had come to give to all.
It was a task most daunting, but multitudes would heed His call.
For Him there would be little rest, for time was much too short.
Too soon He'd have to leave them, His path must not abort.

Though they might run and hide, when the going got too rough,
it would not be too long before they understood enough.
And when the right time came, then eleven would return
and pledge their lives to Christ, for in their hearts, His passion burned.

They would choose when Judas left, another worthy to receive
the command to go and tell the world of what it should believe.
Now throughout all the centuries, the love of Christ is told
through the Holy Spirit's calling by believers brave and bold.

Doubts may come, but doubts can leave, our Father is forgiving,
and longs for us to share His Light as long as we are living.
From generation, to generation, as we pass His love along,
sinners come to Jesus, and then pass along His song.

God is love, above all else, His love will not be hidden!
Satan can try with all His might, but His doom's already written.
We are God's new disciples, we carry on His holy light,
For as long as we are living, we will not give up His fight!

Sometimes we each might falter, or stumble on our way,
but Christ will always have for us the strength we need to stay.
Pray for His love and understanding, He'll guide each path as it goes. He will infuse in us the passion He gave the first twelve men He chose.

...Jesus saith unto them, "Fill the waterpots with water." And they filled them up to the brim. And He saith unto them, "Draw out now and bare unto the governor of the feast." and they bare it...John 2: 7, 8 KJV

Water Into Wine

Before Christ started down His path to save the lost of man,
He went with Mary to a wedding feast taking place in Cana land.
Full of laughter and delight, all were having a great time,
until the host discovered he was running out of wine.

Mary came to Jesus, and asked what He could do.
He told His mother, quietly, His time was not yet due.
But Mary was insistent, told the servants, "Do His will".
He had them gather empty barrels with water to be filled.

Jesus turned that water into the finest wine.
The wedding feast continued, and merrily they dined.
Of the miracles Christ performed, this was just one small spark.
Jesus soon would bring God's light into a world gone dark.

...In the Temple He found people selling cattle, sheep, and doves. He saw others sitting at tables, exchanging different kinds of money. Jesus made a whip out of cords and forced all of them, both the sheep and cattle, to leave the Temple...Jesus answered them, "Destroy this temple and I will build it again in three days...(But the temple Jesus meant was his own body.....John 2: 14, 15, 19, & 20 NCV...There was a man of the Pharisees, named Nicodemus, a ruler of the Jews: The same came to Jesus by night, and said unto him, Rabbi, we know that thou art a teacher come from God: for no man can do these miracles that thou doest, except God be with him.....John 3: 1,2 KJV...And this is the condemnation, that Light has come into the world, and men loved darkness rather than Light, because their deeds were evil... John 3: 19 KJV

Son Of Man, Light of the World, King Upon God's Throne

Jesus came to bring His light to a world that had grown dim.
From Cana to Capernaum, and on to Jerusalem.
After arriving at the temple, Christ found people making trade
in the house built for His Father, and the holy ones who prayed.

He made a scourge of small cords, and drove them all away,
for respect was due His Father, not bargains made for pay.
Upon seeing Jesus do this, the Jews all gathered 'round,
and asked by what authority did He tear their tables down?

Greed was ruling in their hearts, not their inner love for God.
That He should come and do this thing, to them seemed rather odd.
Jesus said their temple could be destroyed, and in three days,
He could raise it up again: at this the leaders were amazed.

It had taken forty and six years to build a place so grand!
But Jesus did not mean the building, nor did He mean the land.
He was talking of His body, the real temple of the Lord.
Later His disciples would recall these words Christ swore.

Religious leaders scoffed at this, but people gathered 'round
and many started to believe in this Teacher they had found.
They praised His name and followed Him everywhere He went.
They longed for all He promised, felt from God He must be sent.

Came to Him in the dark of night, a leader of the Pharisees.
"Rabbi, God must be with you to do such things as these."
When Jesus answered Nicodemus, "Ye must be born again."
Nicodemus was quite baffled, for he did not understand.

He thought this was impossible and asked so very bold,
"How can a man be born again if he is already old?
How can one re-enter a mother's womb a second time?"
This was too complicated to be grasped within his mind.

Again Jesus exclaimed to him, "Ye must be born again,
but of water and the holy spirit, not as another man.
As religious leaders of my people, this much you should see.
For does not always the wind blow wherever it may please?

You hear it's sound and feel it's touch, but this you cannot tell:
from whence it came, or where it goes, or whereby it must dwell.
It is the same for everyone who of the Spirit is re-born.
You believe in what you see, but heaven's message leaves you torn?

No one has gone to heaven yet, and none till now came down.
Here you see the Son of Man, and yet you put Him down?
Only through belief in Me, can man with the Lord abide.
Accept these words I teach you, and cast your doubt aside.

For God so loved the world, He gave His one and only Son,
that all who would believe in Him, would have old lives undone.
A new life would begin in them, a life of love and grace.
A life that would give mercy as I give in My Father's place.

A life that after death will rise forever to abide.
Where God will reign in peace and love; there too I will reside.
Light has come into the world, but darkness is man's plight,
unless that man gives up his sins, and comes into God's Light.

Evil truly hates the Light, will do all it can to halt
Man-kind from believing all the things thus far I've taught.
I am the Way, the Truth, the Light, that to you has been sent.
No one comes unto the Father unless in My name he repents.

Many will not call the Light, for fear their deeds be known,
but those who will accept the Light, will see the true path shown.
Those who come unto Me, will find the path they seek
will make them meek and humble, but will not make them weak.

Strength and courage shall abide, and grace for every need.
They have only to choose My way, then plant again my seed.
To go and tell all that they meet that I will pay the price.
I am the Light come to the world, to meet love's sacrifice."

So Jesus and His disciples went on into the countryside,
teaching and performing miracles, as with others they'd abide.
Near and far the fame of Christ was spoken of with wonder,
as evil ways were brought to light and then thrown all asunder.

Many people now were choosing the path that Jesus taught.
No longer in the throes of fear and doubt would they be caught.
The Father loves the Son, has placed all within His hands.
It was to be left to Christ, according to the God's plans.

Forgiveness was within man's reach, and love as was unknown.
In all the centuries left of time, the quest of Christ has grown.
The seed He planted in man's heart, passed to each generation,
has united all who would believe; this was planned before creation.

God the Father, Christ the Son, in all unity and love,
are joined with the Holy Spirit God sent to us from above.
These three in one, the God-Head, is the pathway we should choose,
to lead us back into God's heart that His grace we may not lose.

For all will come a judgment day, a time to face the life we chose.
Did we accept His gift of love or too long did we dose?
If waiting for tomorrow and tomorrow never comes,
will we reap the lake of fire, or live forever with God's Son?

The choice is for each one to make, please do not wait too long!
The chance might come too swiftly and then alas be gone!
Here's praying you will join me in the jubilation chorus
that will honor with sweet praise the One upon the throne before us.

Jehovah, God of Israel, and all nations in the world,
is waiting for the choice we make, His love has been unfurled.
One only need accept the Light He sent to take our place
upon the cross of Calvary that we might accept His grace.

Forgiven not by what we do, or what we might proclaim.
Forgiven by His grace alone, a gift through Jesus' name.
Reunited then forever, with our Father we will live.
Give praise to Him for Jesus and all that Christ did give.

All glory, laude and honor, to Jesus Christ belong,
for God our Father was the one to place Jesus on His throne.
The Son was in the Father, the Father in the Son
And through the Holy Spirit the three will rule as one.

Son of God, Light of the World, King upon God's throne,
Jesus waits for each of us to choose Him as our own.
Thank you, Father, for the Son in whom You placed your Light.
Thank you, Jesus for the chance to choose Your life so right.

...Righteous Father, though the world does not know You, I know You and they know that You have sent Me. I have made You known to them, and will continue to make You
known in order that the love You have for Me may be in them and that I Myself may be in them...John 17: 24 – 26 NIV

What News This?

Jesus traveled through Samaria, and had stopped at Jacob's well.
He asked a woman for a drink, and much to her did tell.
At first she was surprised that He, a Jew to her would speak.
Hatred ruled between their clans, good will between them weak.
Still, Jesus had a message of living water she would need.
After hearing all He spoke to her, she left with joyous speed.
She went back to her village, told others all she had received.
They came to see Him for themselves, soon they too did believe.

Christ traveled on to Galilee, and into Nazareth town,
and the news about His ministry was spreading all around.
He taught and preformed miracles, almost everywhere He went.
Yet Nazareth would not believe He was the one their God had sent.
He traveled on into Capernaum, and the surrounding countryside.
By lake, by sea, by grains of field, often with sinners to abide.

With rich, with poor, with all He'd share the message of God's love.
He told them all about God's mercy, and forgiveness from above.

Scribes and teachers of Jewish law held power in their hands.
So they kept their eyes and ears on Him so they could lay their plans.
The Pharisees were watching, had leaders listening to His call.
They wondered how the people believed He came from God at all.
They could not lose their power, He would have to be proved wrong!
But His sway over the multitudes grew everyday more strong.
Fame about His teachings, and all the miracles He could do
brought all different kinds of people to hear His message true.

The Pharisees grew jealous as Jesus spoke of things to come.
How Jewish leaders were unfaithful to things that needed to be done.
The leaders did not like how crowds would follow, and believe,
or how the people praised His name, as healing they'd receive.
So leaders watched with diligence, that they might soon find a way
to lure the people back to themselves, away from Jesus' sway.
The message Christ was teaching, leaders felt blasphemed their laws.
They claimed to know the Jewish laws they studied best of all!

But Jesus was not interested in the laws as scribes proclaimed.
He wanted God's laws spoken true, not changed to suit their fame.
The Pharisees and scribes now always did their very best
to change the way God spoke the laws, according to their test.
Christ had not come here to destroy, but to build the laws back up.
He came to show all man-kind the living water of God's cup.
He came to heal God's children, who were lost in the grip of sin.
He came to quell the darkness, to let His Father's love seep in.

He came to bring the good news, God's plan of sweet salvation.
He came to bring God's Light into the dark of His own nation.
Though some Jews might not accept Him, He would give His news to all.
He knew everyone was welcome to accept His Father's call.
People saw His many miracles, how so many sick were healed.
Acceptance came for those believing in the truth He had revealed.
Not so for those who watched concerned, their own power would dim,
because of all the wonder and the trust crowds placed in Him.

Multitudes today will not believe why Jesus came.
They doubt, ignore, stay busy, will not seek His precious name.
Only through God's Holy Spirit will any come into His fold.
Yet how can they believe His love, if His message is not told?
Jesus gave to His disciples one last command for all to keep.
He said that if we loved Him, we should feed all of God's sheep.

The message was so urgent, it was repeated time and again.
We, His true believers need to stoke the fire and fan.

To spread to all the nations, all the people everywhere,
the message of His cross and the resurrection all may share.
His ministry must continue, until He comes back through the clouds,
to gather up God's children with His trumpets blowing loud.
The dead in Christ will rise to meet Him, joyfully within the air.
True believers too will leave for the mansions He's prepared.
Search the book of Revelation, and there all will be revealed.
Tribulation or salvation, it shows how man's fate is sealed.

The victory is already won and Christ will rule supreme!
The devil has already lost, no matter what his scheme.
He may rule the world for just a while, but he himself is fooled.
Christ eventually will send him to where the fiery lake is pooled.
There Satan will be burning throughout all eternity,
along with all the others who refused the Father's seed.
What will be your choice in life, which path will you choose?
Eternally to burn and thirst for the good news you refused?

Will you knock upon the door of faith, to be accepted at His gate.
Will you be welcomed in the arms of love, or revel in the devil's hate?
It really is that simple, won't you just accept God's love.
This was His only purpose in sending Jesus from above.
Satan will change your destination, without ever being seen.
You won't even know he's working, through his hatred that's so keen.
God has the plan of true salvation, where all eternity can be given.
Believe in Jesus' resurrection, and you too shall then be risen.

What news this? Will you refuse without giving faith a glance?
Or will you take the time to seek salvation's only chance?
The good news can't be told enough, or repeated too many times.
Come accept, I beg of you, you'll find a life that is sublime.
Eternity is a goal so grand, but that's not all you will receive.

By choosing to accept His love, by simply choosing to believe,
you will find more peace, more joy; so much more of everything.
Come now to God's alter, accept His love sweet and supreme.

I will be praying for you, as Christ did at Gethsemane.
Remember before we were born, to the Father He did plea,
He wants our lives to be His own, accept who He truly was.
Search the Scriptures, you will find He holds new life for us.
Reach out and grab the love of God, it cannot be stressed enough!
God is waiting patiently for you to call upon His love.
Faith is the substance of things not seen, accept it in your heart.
Christ has already paid the cost, already done His part.

The rest is now friend left to you, don't wait 'til it's too late.
His love is there just for the taking, why not throw wide the gate?
Prayers can work miracles, Jesus prayed and I do too,
that you will accept His message, His grace, His love so true.
Then united we all can be, in eternity above,
to live forever with the One who sacrificed His love.
Then forever we will sing sweet praises to His name.
All glory, laud and honor give, only He deserves such fame.

...Jesus went through Galilee, teaching in their synagogues, preaching the good news of the kingdom, and healing every disease and sickness among the people. News about Him spread all over Syria, and people brought to Him all who were ill with various diseases, those suffering severe pain, the demon possessed, those having seizures, and the paralyzed, and He healed them....Matthew 4:23, 24 NIV... And the Pharisees went forth, and straightway took counsel with the Herodians against Him, how they might destroy Him...Mark 3: 6 KJV

The Ministry of Christ

As Christ began His teachings, His wisdom overcame
doubts and fears and hateful hearts; word spread about His fame.
Many in the crowds that came had illness and disease,
and asked of Jesus if He could in some way their pain ease.

He healed the blind, made well those ill, embraced the lost, the torn;
made lame to walk and dumb to talk, all evil He did scorn.
He cast out devil spirits, and healed upon the Sabbath day.
Which made religious leaders mad, they were jealous of Christ's sway.

They didn't like all the attention, this so-called Teacher was receiving.
They wanted all the glory and they did not mind deceiving.
They tried to trick the Savior, prove Him wrong and cause mistakes.
Christ knew just what they wanted, He knew how high the stakes.

He stood firm within the teaching that He had come to do,
often using parables to help them see the message true.
Near and far His fame did spread, and multitudes would come.
They longed to hear, to see, to learn of Jesus' new Kingdom.

He taught them constantly of love and at the Sermon on the Mount,
He told how the Father blessed them in too many ways to count.
Sometimes as the crowds grew larger, they oft had naught to eat.
Jesus often fed them, a miracle in itself complete.

On came to Him for mercy, more sick, more blind, more lame.
Throughout all of Judea, tales of miracles brought Him fame.
Patiently He healed each one, no matter what their plight,
whether physical or spiritual, Jesus always made it right.

Never before had they been told of a love that ran so strong
that it could ward off evil, and bring to hearts new song.
How the Master did it, they might not understand,
but still they sought the blessings of His loving, gentle hand.

Crowds gathered all around Him, wherever Jesus went.
The disciples would be weary, feeling their strength spent.
Jesus kept on healing, and teaching tirelessly it seemed.
He knew His time was short, too many yet to be redeemed.

He had so much to teach them, lessons He had yet to share,
and before too much time would pass, one miracle beyond compare.
Defeat would lay at Satan's feet, our Lord knew what lay ahead.
The cost of sin He'd pay in full, for man no fear to dread.

Through His own resurrection, Christ would live eternally.
By choosing to believe in Him, forever so can we.
Of all the miracles Christ performed, none could be so grand
as reaching our eternal home to take Christ by the hand.

Then too, with His disciples and the angels we will sing:
eternal praises to our Lord, our rock, our risen King.
Only joyful, faithful hearts will shine in Paradise,
and love will rule forevermore as we abide in Christ.

...But I tell you who hear me: Love your enemies, do good to those who hate you, bless those who curse you, pray for those who mistreat you...Do to others as you would have them do to you. ...Luke 6: 27, 28, & 31 NIV...Therefore everyone who hears these words of Mine and puts them into practice is like a wise man who built his house on the rock.
  ...Matthew 7: 24 NIV

Jesus Speaks of Love

"Come let me teach of love to all, kindness to one another.
"If one smites you on your cheek, then turn to them the other.
Do good to those who hate you, those who curse or abuse too.
Treat your neighbor as yourself, as you wish they'd treat you.

Judgment should not be yours to give, to show mercy is your due.
Then you will not be judged for all the wrong things that you do.
To condemn means you're not loving, as I have every day.
Forgiveness from within the heart, that is the Father's way.

With the measure that you meet, so will it be for you.
Trust in God to judge, condemn, for that's My Father's due.
Why seek the speck of sawdust that lies in another's eye?
Who gave you the authority, to pick, to peck, to pry?

Do not be called a hypocrite, tend only to your life.
There's plenty wrong with each of you, why poke at other's strife?
Good trees do not bear bad fruit, so then why should ye?
Hearts must glow with constant love, not hate or jealous greed.

Lay down your own foundations, with faith your solid rock.
Do not wander needlessly, let your hearts on Me be locked.
Then when the storms of life arise, let faith in your place stand.
Let My love be your shelter; nothing takes you from My hand.

For I am the Good Shepherd and I always know My flock,
and My flock answers to My voice, My leadership is locked.
Believe in all I say to you, reap the harvest that I give.
I tell these things to save you, that a better life you'll live.

Concentrate on what I teach, on the love that all can share.
Let others see how faith in Me has taught you how to care.
Then when I have departed, I'll still live within your heart.
Do as I have taught you, and try to keep the world apart.

The ways of worldly living, have not a thing to do with Me.
My Kingdom is forever, and only I can set you free.
No man cometh to the Father, except He come through Me.
No other pathway can be found, no matter what you see.

I am the Way, the Truth, the Light, I pass my love to you.
Only forgiveness of sin saves, and that only I can do!
What more can I give to you? Will My life be enough?
I lay it freely down for you, so great for you my love.

Why do you call me "Lord, Lord", yet listen not to Me?
I am the Rock you're seeking, how can you this not see?
I will not tarry here much longer, my fate's already set.
How many times will you listen, yet not the message get?

Come unto me all who labor, are weary, beaten, torn.
Let Me become your own salvation, all ye lost, sad and forlorn.
My love's here for the taking, to you it will not be denied.
Won't you accept who I must be, and in My love abide?"

Again, I must remind you not to cast that judgment stone,
unless you have no faults to claim that are your very own.
Again I say to judge not, for in judging you will be,
casting only on yourself, the corrections man-kind needs.

Again I tell you: be the friend, that you'd have others be.
Seek not faults, forgive those found, most unconditionally.
Let Me deal with judgment, for this is My royal due.
My Father gave this right to Me, My judgment is most true.

When I tell you feed my sheep, I'm wanting you to share,
all the love the Father gives, take time to love and care.
If you follow My example, and love as I have loved,
that love will not bear judgment, leave that to your Lord above.

Spend not your time in finding fault with others that you see.
More precious to me are the hours in which you share my seed.
Go and tell the world you meet, of the love that I have taught.
Spend your time more wisely, loving others as you ought.

I came not to condemn the world, but to show the Father's Light.
I came down to remind you all, the cost of sinful plight.
My Father's love is as no other, He has sent it down to you.
Trust in what I came to share, trust in Our love so true.

...And there followed Him great multitudes of people from Galilee, and from Decapolis, and from Jerusalem, and from Judea and from beyond Jordan...Matthew 4:25 KJV...But so much the more went there a fame abroad of Him: and great multitudes came together to hear, and to be healed by Him of their infirmities...Luke 5:15 KJV

Love Reaches Across All Boundaries

From Jerusalem to Samaria, He traveled on to Galilee.
From Galilee to Nazareth, back to Capernaum, traveled He.
By rivers, lakes, the mountainsides, through villages and towns,
He traveled on by foot, by boat, as crowds gathered all around.
A woman in Samaria, whom He met at Jacob's well
Was surprised He'd even speak to her, but He had much to tell.
Between Samaritans and Jews, there dwelled a lot of hate.
Jesus came for all man-kind, none would He isolate.

He told her of the living water, He alone could share.
She ran to tell her village; they rushed back to see Him there.
They too became believers, asked Christ to stay a while.
He tarried shortly, left for Nazareth and taught there without guile.
Yet Nazareth rejected Him and the words He had to say.
They drove Him from their village, so He simply walked away.
In Capernaum, He healed lepers and made the lame to walk.
Forgave men of their evil sins, thus the scribes began to balk.

Jesus could not forgive man's sin, of this they were quite sure!
Only Jehovah could forgive, He must be the devil's lure.
He could not be the Son of God, He could not take their place.
They knew the law better than He, how dare He show His face!
Yet His fame spread through the land, as wildfire through dry leaves.
Though He wanted quiet miracles, news spread quickly on each breeze.
Through every town and village, how could they halt His fame?
It seemed to know no boundaries, how quickly spread His flame.

As they pondered what to do, Christ moved forth to spread the news.
The Father loved mankind so much, He sent His Son to pay man's dues.
The Jews would be the first He called, but Christ would not stop there.
The message was for all of man, to show how much God cared.
Gentiles too would be received; the cross was for all nations.
That is why man's life now should be filled with celebrations!
The debt of sin's been paid in full, for all who want God's Light!
The resurrection of the Christ will call us all to flight.

Not only can all lives now bask in the warmth of Jesus' love,
all nations can look forward to their home with Christ above.
Eternity can now be claimed no matter from what clan.
There are no boundaries that can hold man from the Savior's stand.
The devil tries still every day, just as the scribes once did.
But death could not be the victor, once Jesus made His bid.
O death where lies thy victory? In the shadow of the cross?
The Light of God withdrew the dark; sin's victory is lost!

Just as Jesus rose back then, so will all who dare believe.
No boundaries will stop His call, to those He will receive.
To deny the Son of God, is to deny the Lord of all.
One day every knee will bow down at the Savior's call.
One day all will know beyond the shadow of a doubt,
That Jesus is man's saving grace; God's children shout it out!
Across the nation's boundaries, His love reaches all who hear.
According to God's purpose, His love brings all of man-kind near.

...The centurion heard of Jesus and sent some elders of the Jews to Him, asking Him to come and heal his servant. When they came to Jesus, they pleaded earnestly with Him, "This man deserves to have you do this, because he loves our nation and has built our synagogue." So Jesus went with them. He was not far from the house when the centurion sent friends to say to Him: "Lord don't trouble yourself, for I do not deserve to have You come under my roof. That is why I did not even consider myself worthy to come to you. But say the word, and my servant will be healed....When Jesus heard this, He was amazed at him, and turning to the crowd following Him, He said, "I tell you, I have not found such great faith even in Israel...Luke 7: 3 – 7 & 9 NIV

The Faith of The Centurion

Jesus traveled with His disciples throughout all the land.
Teaching of the Father's love for all of fellowman.
Fame about what Christ could do spread to every town.
Everywhere that Jesus went, the crowds gathered all around.
They listened as He taught them; saw the miracles He could do.
Was He really the Messiah, had the prophecies come true?

A centurion heard the story, sent elders to seek Him out.
For he had a servant dying that he cared so much about.
People told the Master how worthy this centurion,
how well he served the people, all for them that he had done.
Jesus was quite willing to do as He was asked,
but the centurion felt unworthy of such a loving task.

If Jesus would but say the words, his servant would be healed.
Jesus had not seen such faith in all of Israel.
Christ told him healing would be done just as the man had asked.
Sure enough as Jesus said, in health the servant basked.
If only faith as sure as that centurion proclaimed
would dwell in all of us today, how great would be God's name.

Why do we have to see first, before we can believe?
Why can we not accept on faith just what we might receive?
People before us have believed; healing was theirs to claim.
Why can we not have such faith, all in the Savior's name?
No one needs to feel unworthy, for Christ does not agree,
or He would not have died for us with love beyond degree.

All our sins He bore alone, to the Hill of Calvary.
He suffered deepest agony: the price to set us free.
I choose to believe in Him, I pray that you will too.
Call upon the Savior's name; you'll see what He can do.
His love is waiting for you, why don't you seek Him out.
Can't you see that loving you is what He's all about?

He gave His life to prove it, will you simply turn away?
Why not accept His gift of love, why not accept today?
Why let fear or doubts arise, why tarry any longer?
Why live just in the present, why not let yourself be stronger?
Don't wait until tomorrow; just think of what you'll lose!
I pray such faith as that centurion; will be the life you'll choose.

And if that choice has been made, already in your life,
how sweet our praise to Him must sound, as we face every strife.
How wonderful, how marvelous, that we can call His name.
Soak in His love and mercy as His promises proclaim.
Great is Thy faithfulness unto all, new each morn we can see,
There is no greater love to find than what He gives for free.

...And, behold, there came a man named Jairus, and he was a ruler of the synagogue: and he fell down at Jesus' feet, and besought Him that He would come into His house: For he had one only daughter, about twelve years of age, and she lay a-dying. But as he went, the people thronged Him. And a woman having an issue of blood twelve years, which had spent all her living upon physicians, neither could be healed of any, Came behind Him, and touched the border of His garment: and immediately her issue of blood stanched...While He yet spake, there cometh one for the ruler of the synagogue's house, saying to him, Thy daughter is dead; trouble not the Master...And all wept, and bewailed her: but He said, "Weep not; she is not dead, but sleepeth. And they laughed Him to scorn, knowing that she was dead. And He put them all out, and took her by the hand, and called, saying, "Maid, arise."...Luke 8: 41 –44, 49,52 - 54 KJV

When Two Miracles Converged

Came to Christ in sorrow, a man whose child was dying.
He asked if Christ would come to the place where she was lying.
Then if Christ would but touch her, the illness would be gone.
Jesus left to follow him but He did not leave alone.

Because He had been teaching, the crowd still gathered 'round,
and followed Him to see if any healing could be found.
A woman soon reached in her hand, oh just to touch His hem,
and Jesus quickly felt His virtue moving out from Him.

He wondered who had touched Him, but so many 'round Him poked.
All wondered how He felt one touch, of whom the Savior spoke?
The woman, though much frightened, stepped bravely forth and said,
"I am the one who touched you, oh but now I shake with dread.

I hope you will forgive me, I thought if I just touched your gown,
from this awful blood disease, your healing could be found."
"Thy faith has healed thy illness," was Jesus quick reply.
"Go live thy life in peace and health, no reprimand have I."

Before Christ reached the Father's home, came news that brought great pain,
"Jairus, bother not the Lord, for now it is in vain.
Your daughter has already died, His help has come too late."
To which the Savior quickly said, "She lies at slumber's gate".
Taking the parents and three disciples, He went on to where she lay,
and speaking to her, raised her from within death's dreadful sway.

All there rejoiced and marveled, although they had laughed before.
Jesus knew much more would come, before He could right wrong's score.
All the miracles He still accomplished, cannot be written down,
for too many came unto Him, to seek His mercies all around.
They could not doubt the things they saw there right before their eyes.
Yet, how quickly they would soon forget, would doubt Him and despise.

Would come the day their leaders would turn their praise to hate.
Would come the day the people turned, their wonder to abate.
Jesus knew it all was coming, but He still had work to do.
He still performed more miracles, told more of His message true.
Just search the scriptures, you will find, how faithful Christ would be.
How faithful still, He is today, and throughout eternity.

What more could we ask for, in a Savior, faithful, true?
What greater message could there be, than this man's love for you.
I promise you dear Father, that I too will faithful be,
to tell as best I'm able, of Thy love for all to see.
By word of mouth, by written pen, in any way I can:
That Jesus is our risen King, who died for all of man.

...And a great multitude followed Him, because they saw His miracles which He did on them that were diseased...When Jesus then lifted up His eyes, and saw a great company come unto Him, He saith unto Philip, "Whence shall we buy bread, that these may eat?"

...One of His disciples, Andrew, Simon Peter's brother, saith unto Him, "There is a lad here, which hath five barley loaves, and two small fishes: but what are they among so many?...John 6: 2,5,8 & 9 KJV

What Are You Among So Many?

More than once the Savior saw more crowds than men could count.
Yet He had so much to teach them, He welcomed all unto His fount.
Many times His messages of truth would last all day,
and physical hunger of the crowds would often His heart sway.

The disciples would be faithless, would wonder how to feed them all.
Jesus never worried for on His Father He could call.
In the feeding of five thousand, of men alone, not counting others,
the disciples with Him doubted how Christ could feed their brothers.

Can you see the stress that's written, on each disciple's face?
He has already taught and healed them, and all with loving grace.
It now was time, or so they thought, to send them all away.
And yet, He planned to feed them? Impossible they'd say.
They were looking at material cost, not delving into faith.
What their Master sought, disciples met with wondering scathe.
"Stop, they told the Master, "we have naught for them to eat."
Till one young boy gave up his lunch to lay at Jesus feet.

Five small loaves of barley bread, and two small fish, no more.
"One small basket cannot feed them all," disciples swore.
See their faith so shaky, heeding not the Lord's intent.
Such contrast of views, our Lord would easily circumvent.

Looking up to heaven, Jesus blessed the food with grace.
Dividing it among the crowd, soon all there were amazed.
When the meal was over, and leftovers gathered 'round:
twelve baskets filled with fragments lay gathered on the ground.

They called Him "Master", "Teacher", so many starting to believe.
What do you call Him, now, today, what blessings to receive.
Do you think that He's too busy, to ask the Father for your grace?
Do you think He will do nothing because He's not seen face to face?

That young boy had faith to believe in what the Christ could do!
If you have faith in who He is, He'll do the same for you.
Do you think He does not know you in a world so multiplied?
I believe He knows us all, to each His love can be applied!

What are you among so many? He died for you, why can't you see?
Anything that you might offer Him, can be changed to all you need.
Just call on Him, He's waiting, longs to love you and to bless.
He'll multiply and give you more than you could ever guess.

You may thing your basket's much too small, for Him to see at all.
Nay, friend, it only needs your faith, so why not seek and call?
What are you among so many? As He looks, He just sees you.
He's ready, willing, able, to send you His blessings too.

...Immediately He told His followers to get into the boat and go ahead of Him across the lake. He stayed there to send the people home. After He had sent them away, He went by Himself up into the hills to pray. It was late, and Jesus was there alone. By this time, the boat was already far away from land. It was being hit by waves, because the wind was blowing against it. Between three and six o'clock in the morning, Jesus came to them, walking on the water. When His followers saw Him walking on the water, they were afraid. They said, "It's a ghost!" and cried out in fear. But Jesus quickly spoke to them, "Have courage! It is I. Do not be afraid." Peter said, "Lord, if it is really You, then command me to come to You on the water." Jesus said, "Come." And Peter left the boat and walked on the water to Jesus. But when Peter saw the wind and the waves, he became afraid and began to sink. He shouted, "Lord, save me!" Immediately Jesus reached out His hand and caught Peter. Jesus said, "Your faith is small. Why do you doubt?...Mathew 14: 22 – 31 NCV

Take A Walk On Water

In Matthew is a story of faith lost because of doubt.
How Peter trusted just a bit, then let his faith fall out.
Christ had sent his followers on ahead across the sea,
while He stayed behind to pray, alone as He could be.

In the early light of morn, He saw them far from shore.
He stepped out upon the water as if it were a floor.
He walked upon the water to His friends inside the boat.
They thought they saw a vision, He seemed as if to float.

Fear and doubt arose in them as Jesus came so near.
Surely it must be a ghost, they cried out in their fear!
Jesus quickly spoke to them, "Fear not! For it is I."
They recognized their Master, as He gave them this reply.

Peter said, "Lord, if it's You, command for me to come."
Jesus did, Peter stepped out, walked just as Christ had done.
Then Peter let his focus from the Master slip away.
He saw the rocking waves and doubted in the Master's sway.

In fear he cried, "Lord! Save me!" Jesus reached to him with hand.
"Your faith is small," the Master said, "Why did you doubt faith's stand?"
Why do we doubt even today? Why tremble we in fear?
Did not the Master tell us that He was always near?

Though we try hard to have faith in what we should believe,
sometimes doubts still will slither in, to trick us and deceive.
This doubt comes from Satan, on our weakness he relies.
Our faith in Christ he wants to quench, he strikes at us with lies.

If we doubt the Savior and the promises He brings,
into the dark of doubt and fear, we much too easy fling.
Trust is such a simple thing, yet oft so hard to share.
We want to be so sure of things before we ever dare.

What will happen? What will come? How can we be sure?
Oh how easy it can be to fall for Satan's lure.
Doubt and fear unsettles us, yet it lives in each and all.
The only way to conquer each? Trust in the Savior's call.

We're not the first to slip and fall into the devil's web.
Even the apostles often let their courage ebb.
How many times it happens, this doubt that sneaks right in?
How many times we're challenged, on ourselves we must depend?

Jesus cries, "Come thou to Me! For I will see you through."
Still we ponder, moan and groan, but what more must Christ do?
How many times do we ourselves, let our focus slip away
from the very One who always has the grace to stay.

Why do we doubt and fear so much, yes, it happens to us all.
We fret and worry, tremble and cry, we stumble and we fall.
Christ is always there to catch us, with His grace, fulfill each need.
Why is it we still worry, when faith in Him should be our creed.

We too can walk on water, without ever sinking down,
as long as we have trust in Him and His love that abounds.
His love everlasting, His mercy and His grace
are more powerful a tonic than any doubts or fears we face.

We all may be so undeserving, yet His mercy's always there,
because He has believed in us, with all His love to share.
In Christ we must place our lives, our hearts, to stronger be.
For His grace is sufficient for anything in life we see.

Thank You Jesus, Savior, that on you we can rely.
Thank You for forgiveness, when upon your name we cry.
Thank You, precious Savior, You do not accuse or blame.
Thank You for the love You give, when we are filled with shame.

Thank You for your courage, whenever storm clouds settle in.
Thank You for your mercy, You are the place we should begin.
Forgive us when we stumble, let not our focus slip or slide.
Forgive us when we're weakest, help our love in You abide.

Let Your love light bloom forth even in the darkest night.
When we call upon Your name, remove from us our fright.
Help us to step forward upon those waves of doubt.
Help us walk upon the stormy seas that toss our lives about.

Praise to the Father, to the Son, to the Comforter that was sent.
For all the courage and the strength on each of us you've spent.
Walk on water? Impossible? Not when the Savior has your back.
Go to Him and ask of Him, have faith in what you lack.

He will answer, every time, don't let doubt make you sink.
Believe in all His mercy, let Him fill you to the brink.
He gave His life to prove His love, all you need do is ask.
His mercy will come right in you, to fulfill any task.

Don't forget to thank Him, for His strength, courage, and grace.
You can take that walk on water, just keep your focus on His face.
Take a walk on water, take a walk in His sweet love.
Remember that sweet praise to Christ, pleases our God above.

... "How is it you don't understand that I was not talking to you about bread? But be on your guard against the yeast of the Pharisees and Sadducees. Then they understood that He was not telling them to guard against the yeast used in bread, but against the teaching of the Pharisees and Sadducees....Matthew 16: 11 & 12...NIV... "Woe to the world because of the things that cause people to sin! Such things must come, but woe to the man through whom they come!...Mathew 18: 7 NIV...Jesus replied, "And you experts in the law, woe to you, because you load people down with burdens they can hardly carry, and you yourselves will not lift one finger to help them...Woe to you experts in the law, because you have taken away the key to knowledge. You yourselves have not entered, and you have hindered those who were entering."...Luke: 11: 46 & 52...I tell you, whoever acknowledges Me before men, the Son of man will also acknowledge him before the angels of God. But he who disowns Me before men will be disowned before the angels of God....Luke 12: 8 & 9 NIV

What Yeast This?

Jesus came into the world to uphold true His Father's laws.
The Pharisees had twisted these around to suit their cause.
Jesus warned them many times to change the way they lived.
He blessed the things they didn't do, not what they liked to give.

Justice, love and honor, they'd brush casually aside.
In their hearts no mercy, grace, or cleanliness did abide.
They would load down the ones who'd listen, with half-truths and with lies.
Though they appeared so faithful, they all were living in disguise.

On the outside it appeared as if their teachings were quite pure.
But what lay in their inner hearts caused men a false allure.
What they taught the people might seem true them.
Only Jesus taught the true law, as the Father gave to Him.

Their yeast Jesus said, would give rise to evil ways.
Their yeast taught of selfishness, of darkness and decays.
The Father sent the Son to teach the laws as they'd been written.
The Pharisees had changed them for by power they'd been bitten.

Woe be to all the Savior said, who led others astray.
Biblical truth remains the same both then and still today.
"What yeast have ye in thy heart?" Hear the Savior ask?
"What do ye, to benefit the Father's loving task?"

World-wide now religions spread, each with groups of their own.
Man wants to live as man sees fit, with rules that he can spawn.
False prophets, teachers, leaders, everywhere seem to abound.
Teaching man as they see fit, they claim their teachings sound.

"I am the Way, the Truth, the Light." Jesus said it many times.
Only one way is the truth, only one way can be prime.
If we do not take the Bible as God's own written plan,
who might we be influencing or condemning, from His hand.

Who might we be deceiving into complacent attitudes,
when instead we should be giving them God's love and fortitude?
The yeast of each life ferments into all other lives we share.
What might we be giving them, are we living unaware?

The Father has been pleased to offer to His children dear,
a life that's filled with love, with peace and joy so ever near.
He does not want for us to hold that love within ourselves.
He longs for us to pass it on, not hide it within closet shelves.

Who is faithful, who is wise, who tries to do their best?
Will we faithful servants be, or Pharisees who failed the test?
We cannot live the way we should, if the Bible lays in dust.
It must be studied, taught, and loved, God placed in us its trust.

His word is the law that we should follow everyday.
His yeast, the fermentation we need to pass on in His way.
We must beware of how we live, of the lifestyle that we choose.
God forbid that we should cause someone His grace to lose.

All who will deny the Christ, or claim His message false,
will be the ones at judgment time counted among the lost.
Deny not the Savior's love, or He then won't claim you.
Trust Him as the Son of God, sent with His message true.

Let us be a beacon, together joining in the fight
against the evil force who longs to cancel sinners' right.
All have the chance to come to Him, if we get Christ's message out.
All have the chance to learn and live what God is all about.

Let the yeast within us all expand to fill the world.
Let the message of His love be joyfully unfurled.
The Bible is the Word of God, forever may it rise
So every heart can have the chance to gain it's sweet surprise.

What yeast this? Oh, tell it true! The best that it can be!
It's touched the lives of millions, yet has millions more to see.
Father, Son and Holy Ghost, all reaching out to you.
Will you be a Pharisee, or seek His message true?

...And He went through the cities and villages, teaching, and journeying toward Jerusalem. Then said one unto Him, "Lord, are there few that be saved?" And He said unto them, "Strive to enter in at the strait gate: for many, I say unto you, will seek to enter in, and shall not be able...Then shall ye begin to say, "We have eaten and drunk in Thy presence, and Thou hast taught in our streets. But He shall say, I tell you I know you not whence ye are; depart from me, all ye workers of iniquity. There shall be weeping and gnashing of teeth, when ye shall see Abraham, and Isaac, and Jacob, and all the prophets, in the kingdom of God, and you yourselves thrust out...And behold, there are last which shall be first, and there are first which shall be last...O Jerusalem, Jerusalem, which killest the prophets, and stonest them that are sent unto thee; how often would I have gathered thy children together, as a hen doth gather her brood under wings, and ye would not....Luke 13: 22-24, 26-28 & 30 & 34 KJV

Who Will Enter The Heavenly Kingdom?

Rich man, poor man, beggar man thief,
doctor, lawyer, Indian chief.
We said it many times as a child.
Once grown we put it away a while.

Now comes the time that we must ask:
of all the people, which faced the task?
Will race, or color, or sex or creed
determine who or when we're each set free?

If heaven's gate is to be realized,
how hard can it be to win the prize?
Who will win and who will lose?
It all depends on the life you choose.

Being rich won't help, nor will being poor.
A thief won't be welcome at heaven's door.

Education of worldly studies renown
won't win for anyone a victor's crown.

Pretending to be what we are not
will not erase one sinner's spot.
Hypocrisy is not welcome there,
nor the self-centered, no love to share.

Liars, cheaters, breakers of law,
teachers of evil's lusty call.
Those who claim some other god,
or refuse the path that Jesus trod,

none will be welcome, unless they call
for the Savior to save them from it all.
Any sin we commit can be forgiven,
if faith is strong in the Son who is risen.

Only those who truly believe
will gain the greatest prize to receive.
Word of mouth alone will not atone.
Actions speak louder than words alone.

Jesus knocks on every heart's door.
Will you let Him in, your Savior, Lord?
Just to call His name will not be enough,
to enter His kingdom, you must live love.

While works of faith will not suffice,
they show your genuine love for Christ.
Faith without works cannot be approved,
but living faith great mountains have moved.

So trust in Jesus, so pure and true.
Seek out His grace to see us through.

Stay faithful through the Spirit's power.
Trust that He is with us every hour.

Confession cleanses the troubled soul.
He answers all calls, both young and old.
Who will enter the Father's Holy Kingdom?
Only those who willingly to Christ come.

Jesus is the light , the truth God gave
only through His grace can one be saved.
The gates of heaven accept only those
who've made His life the kind they chose.

Everyone who lives, is born to sin
accepting Christ is being born again.
Choose to believe, repent, be saved!
Come enter the kingdom our Father gave.

Rich man, poor man, beggar man thief,
matters not at all if you place belief
in the life Christ gave to save us all;
in the choice you make to heed His call.

No role in life, no race, no creed,
no country, no power has what we need.
The gate may be narrow, but come enter in
through Jesus Christ, our Savior, our Friend.

All will be forgiven if you truly desire
the path of love that will lift you higher.
Repentance, acceptance go hand in hand.
Love Christ and enter His Promise Land.

...Jesus took the Twelve aside and told them, "We are going up to Jerusalem, and everything that is written by the prophets about the Son of Man will be fulfilled. He will be handed over to the Gentiles. They will mock Him, insult Him, spit on Him, flog Him and kill Him. On the third day He will rise again."...Luke 18: 31 – 34 NIV... "For I know the plans I have for you," declares the Lord. "plans to prosper you and not to harm you, plans to give you hope and a future. Then you will call upon me and come to pray to me, and I will listen to you. You will seek me and find me when you seek me with all of your heart."... "I am with you and will save you," declares the Lord.
   ...Jeremiah 29: 11 - 13

What Jesus Knew

In the days of old, prophets told of things to come.
As early as in Genesis was the prediction of the Son.
In this day and time, when predictions are foretold,
it's from psychics or from mediums, or fortune tellers bold.
Some believe and some do not, it is arguable at best.
Yet early prophets always knew, the Bible does attest.
In the Bible, God's true word, everything they warned,
came true through the generations, even now, should not be scorned.

Just as they had predicted, Jesus' birth came true.
Even Christ, Himself, knew all the things that He would do.
He knew His birth was lowly, not in a palace as a King.
As a child of twelve, to temple elders, He would bring
wisdom far beyond His years, in spirit He grew strong.
He knew His life had purpose, to His Father He belonged.
Knew baptism was a must, if the scriptures would come true.
To seek guidance, to be tempted, all of these would be His due.

He longed to give His healing, of the body, mind and soul.
He longed to bring back to man the laws His Father told.
He hungered deeply in His heart to show His Father's love.

Always He would pray for us from sin to rise above.
He knew each road He'd need to take to wash our sins away.
Knew the cost, that He alone would be the One to pay.
More than once He warned His disciples what would be.
Yet they could not understand, the truth they could not see.

Peter denied that Christ, his Lord, should ever pay such price.
Jesus waned that Satan longed to halt God's sacrifice.
Then Satan could have free rein with us all forevermore.
Our Savior did not want death, but He wanted life much more.
Not for His life, would He give in, but for our lives He would.
He meant for all to have the chance to be saved as they should.
He knew He would be praised for all the miracles He would do.
Knew multitudes would follow Him to seek what He claimed true.

He knew His fame would stretch out through every realm of time.
Knew the life He offered was the best of life sublime.
He knew too that the crowd would turn, cry for His crucifixion.
Knew the scribes and Pharisees would play on man's addiction.
Sinful sway is easy, when on the outside looking in.
They tricked the people to believe Christ could not cleanse their sin.
Jesus knew instead of praise, His life would soon be scorned.
Knew that He'd be beaten until His bloodied skin lay torn.

He knew He would be spit upon, ridiculed right in His face.
Yet He carried every bit of this, with purpose and with grace.
He would not defend Himself, to the Father He'd be true.
This was the reason He was born, what He was meant to do.
Who among the whole of man has ever been so strong?
Who among the whole of man ever righted so much wrong?
Would any one of us go forth to take on so much pain,
to spare some strangers from the Lord's most righteous, just disdain?

To Christ we were no strangers, to His heart we were so worth
any pain and suffering He might carry on this earth.

He loved His Father best of all, but His brethren too were cherished.
He knew the cost, accepted all, even if His life was perished.
Still, He knew that He would rise, in three days, live again.
Through His sacrifice, we too, can share in love's eternal span.
Jesus knew, before time was, the things that man must face.
How many times each would be told before accepting grace.

I need no psychic, medium, or fortune teller bold,
to tell me of the wonder that's been told from times of old.
Jesus is my Savior, how I pray He is yours too.
When we meet with Him in glory, we'll learn all that Jesus knew.

For now our lives we must prepare, living in His will.
Before it is too late for our confessions to be spilled.
Judgment day will be too late, the die now must be cast.
Will you stand before His throne, as one who never asked?
Maybe you agree with me, or maybe then you don't.
Maybe this life I try to live is not just what you want.
I'd rather live with hope of heart, heaven as my desire
Than take a chance on misery in the eternal lake of fire.

My heart seeks the Savior, but it seeks for you as well
the hope of peaceful joy and bliss, of which the Bible tells.
Not just for all eternity, but for this life you live now too.
For all that I have gained through Christ, I wish that too for you.
I cannot choose it for you, that choice is yours to make.
Yet I believe without Him, is living with the worst mistake.
I believe what Jesus knew, before time, then and now
Is living in the best of life, He gave His solemn vow.

Father, as I write these words, I pray for all the lost.
Open their eyes and hearts to see how sin carries such cost.
Have mercy, Lord I beg of Thee, let some of all that Jesus knew,
be accepted in their hearts. Please bring them home to You.
So many will not take the time to make the proper choice.
Speak to them, until they hear and come to know Thy voice.

So many Lord will perish, how I wish their hearts would turn,
be filled with Thy Holy Spirit, and for Thee their passion burn.

Your Son knew this was the pathway that all of man should choose.
Let not the business of life cause such hatred and abuse.
Mercy, kindness, one another, should be first in each one's heart.
Each should carry forth Thy love, show their best to do Your part.
Shower Lord, Thy whispers of eternal love, and grace
until they come to know you, come to humbly seek Thy face.
Thank You for Your presence in all that we may do.
Thank You that all that Jesus knew can be known unto us too.
Amen

...Then came the day of Unleavened Bread on which the Passover lamb had to be sacrificed. Jesus sent Peter and John, saying, "Go and make preparations for us to eat the Passover."...Luke 22: 7,8

Making Preparations

Jesus sent His servants on ahead to prepare the way
for His entry into Jerusalem to commend Passover Day.
He gave them clear instructions of what they were to do,
of what to say when questioned; and all He said came true.
He had a clear objective, knew what needed to be done,
to glorify His Father through the glory of the Son.

As Jesus came into the city, upon a borrowed ass,
clothes and palm leaves people threw before Him as He passed.
The Messiah long awaited would halt hated Roman reign.
Loud hosannas, shouts of welcome throughout the city rang.
"Blessed is the one who comes, in the name of our dear Lord."
They all rejoiced, they all sang out with praise of one accord.

The Pharisees were watching in horror and in awe.
Not for Jesus as the Savior, but that the crowd should sing at all.
They had become so jealous; they claimed "twas blasphemy!"
And plotted they together, against this man from Galilee.
Why, He was taking all their power so their anger grew and grew.
They had to stop Him somehow, though they knew not what to do.

Many times had they sent spies, who tried to do their best
to trick our Savior if they could, but Jesus knew their quest.
They questioned Him of taxes, but Jesus said to them:
"Thou render unto Ceasar that which belongs to him."
Sadducees too would try to catch Jesus with their laws.
His wisdom overcame them, into their trap He would not fall.

Then Christ spoke of "show and tell," how Pharisees and scribes
cared more for special privilege, for power and for bribes.
They wanted more the glory; their hearts were filled with pride;
yet justice, faith, and mercy, they still brushed casually aside.
"Woe be unto them," Jesus said, "though appearances seem grand,
'tis not without that holds the key, but the love inside each man."

And though the rich, our Savior saw oft had a lot to give,
Christ favored more the widow's mite, 'twas all she had to live.
To put God first, she gave her all, with devotion and with love,
and that was just the gift desired from the Father up above.
When the scribes knew nothing else that they could ask our Lord,
they plotted even stronger to even up the score.

Then for the cross our Savior tried His disciples to prepare;
by telling of the trials they each would have to bear.
He told them of the mercies they'd need show their fellowman.
No matter what the hardship, they would need the firmest stand.
He warned them to stay righteous, to the scriptures faithful be;
told of future persecutions to those that dared believe.

As they gathered in that upper room, Christ had much on His mind,
knowing this would be the last time with His friends He'd dine.
He knew the pain and suffering too soon He would have to face,
yet each trial and tribulation He would conquer with sweet grace.
Thus Jesus Himself taught us that no greater love is known
than giving one life for another, even if it be your own.

To do His Father's will, would take courage beyond measure.
Yet His sacrifice for all would become life's most precious treasure.
Now each heart prepares its choice, to be or not to be:
child of God with Christ, by grace becoming sinless, free;
or in cahoots with Satan, who's lies are evil chaos bringing.
Which choice brings destruction, which choice joyful singing?

We too have preparations that need to be made now, before,
any one can enter in through heaven's narrow door.
Praise God we have a Savior, who knew what to prepare.
Who knew we needed to return to the Father's love and care.
Come join with me in bringing Jesus' message to the world.
Come help me shower blessings, instead of Satan's tricks unfurled.

Repent! Repent! Hear, John the Baptist, as he boldly called for all
to make straight their pathway to the Lord, to heed the Master's call.
Rejoice! Rejoice! We have the Light, to lead us safely home.
To guide us through life's darkest roads that all of us must roam.
Give thanks! Give thanks! The Father meant before time ever started,
to send to us Savior, that from His love, we'd not be parted.

...After two days was the feast of the Passover, and of unleavened bread: and the chief priests and the scribes sought how they might take Him by craft, and put Him to death...Mark 14:1 KJV

Something To Talk About: The Hearts of The Pharisees

"Did you see when He first came, how they all greeted Him?"
"What can they be thinking! How can they be so dim?"
"Did you hear how they sang praises to His name as if a God?"
"How can they be so stupid as to follow such a sod?"
"They exalt Him as a King, they lift His name on high.
I'm tired of hearing His praise ring up to the sky!"

"He's teaching them, and He's healing them,
why they're putting all their hope in Him!"
"He's telling them new paths to take,
turn the other cheek and love, not hate."
"And from where did all these people come?
How dare they believe He's the Father's Son!"

"We best beware, send out more spies,
if we take care, we'll gain our prize.
Now with the people He may be strong,
but we'll plot and plan; we'll prove Him wrong!"
"Just because He does some tricks! Why that's pure blasphemy!
How dare He tread our sacred ground, this man from Galilee!"

"If we can't trap Him, if He knows our hearts,
then we'll find us a traitor to do our part!"
"Those silly people may dare to believe,
but we've someone in mind who just might deceive."
We can trick, mislead, make the price just right;
but it must be done in the secret of night."

"We'll bide our time 'til the right moment comes.
Into our hands will fall this "proclaimed Son!"
"Let Him teach His precious Father's will,
we will find a way for Him to be killed!"
"Then His victory will become quite sour!
Once again we'll have back all of our power."

"You just wait, you lowly Nazarene,
we will never let them crown you king!"
"We are better than you, we know the law.
We don't believe you come from God at all!"
"Let alone that you are God's own Son.
Wait and see what happens once we are done."

"I can hardly wait to see our victory complete!
Oh how sweet will be this man's defeat!"
"We'll just see how he deals with death's dread sway.
We'll even trick the Romans to stand in His way!"
"And no one will ever put the blame on us.
One again we will have all the people's trust."

"And those stupid Romans, they won't know a thing!
No one will be able to stop our reign!"
Aren't we smart to do it this way?
Serves Him right for trying to steal our sway!"
"Let us go find others that feel this way too,
but keep it quiet! There is much yet to do."

...And when the hour was come, He sat down, and the twelve apostles with Him. And He said unto them, "With desire I have desired to eat this Passover with you before I suffer: For I say unto you, I will not any more eat thereof, until it be fulfilled in the Kingdom of God... Luke 22: 14 – 16 KJV...But I say unto you, I will not drink henceforth of this fruit of the vine, until that day when I drink it new with you in My Father's kingdom...
   Matthew 26: 29 KJV

The Lord's Last Supper

The last supper Jesus would eat with friends upon this earth
would be this one Passover meal, always of greater worth.
As they sat, He told his friends of the sadness that He felt,
for within their very midst, a betrayer of Him dwelt.
One of whom they trusted would betray before the morrow
the very One they loved so much; how deep would be their sorrow.

The disciple's could not believe it, which of them could it be?
They all loved and served the Master, their sin they could not see.
Each in turn would ask Him, but one heart was not sincere.
"Lord is it I? Who could betray? We love You Lord, that's clear.
They could not understand that one of them would dare to spy.
They worked daily right beside Him, how could this be and why?

At last He said it was the one dipping with Him in the dish.
Jesus said, "Go quickly now, fulfill your wicked wish."
Satan had deceived through greed and captured Judas' heart
so Judas quickly got up and made his exit to depart.
Woe be unto the one who would betray the Son of man.
For him the better path would be if life never began.

When Judas left the others did not suspect that it was him.
They thought he had some duty that he must do for them.
Judas was the one who kept the monies that they spent.

He paid the costs of living, perhaps the poor was his intent.
After Judas left them, strife rose again among the men.
Which one would be the greatest among the lot of them?

Even those beloved men would bicker, gripe and groan.
Each one desired the best seat in heaven for his own.
Jesus warned them quickly, they knew not what they asked.
Those decisions were meant only to be His Father's task.
A kingdom was appointed by the Father for His Son.
There they would have a special task that needed to be done.

They all would dine with Him some day at His kingdom's station.
And they alone were chosen to judge the twelve tribes of their nation.
From the first through to the last they'd stand within God's will,
but they would need a servant's heart if His love would be fulfilled.
Christ had come to manhood in a simple, lowly way,
not as a mighty warrior king to conquer sin's dread sway.

Yet conquer evil, this He did, but He conquered it with love
as never seen by man before coming from God above.
He still had much to tell them, in the time left that was short.
He needed to work quickly to build up His kingdom's fort.
Here on earth He could not linger, but His message must be cast
These men would bring His kingdom to fulfillment at long last.

Centuries might unfold but the news must reach to all.
Man must be given one last chance to heed the Master's call.
God in Christ, Christ in God, by their Holy Spirit bound,
Just as we are one in Him, by grace we have been found.
We are His and He is ours, at the Marriage Supper of the Lamb
We will dine forevermore with our Lord, the great I Am.

...I am the good shepherd. The good shepherd lays down his life for the sheep. The hired hand is not the shepherd who owns the sheep. So when he sees the wolf coming, he abandons the sheep and runs away. Then the wolf attacks the flock and scatters it...The reason that my Father loves Me is that I lay down My life - only to take it up again. No one takes it from me, but I lay it down of My own accord. I have authority to lay it down and authority to take it up again. This command I received from My Father...
John 10: 11,12, 17 and 18

Betrayal's Cost

Deep in the Garden of Gethsemane,
our Savior knelt on bended knee.
There, as He lifted His heart in prayer,
three disciples slept without a care.

Jesus brought them along, a vigil to keep,
but right away they fell fast asleep.
They knew not the pain and suffering He'd bear.
Of what was to come, they slept unaware.

'Tis midnight in the garden now,
as sweat drops of blood have wet His brow.
the darkness surrounds Him, He seeks to find
the courage and strength to ease His mind.

He tries to wake His friends who sleep.
Profoundly troubled, His woe runs deep.
Their comfort He seeks, but to no avail.
They can't stay awake. His sadness swells.

All alone He faces what has to be,
no one save the Father to hear His plea.
"Father, I humbly pray to Thee,
if possible, pass this cup from Me.

Yet only dear Father, if it be Thy will.
I remain your servant, destiny to fulfill.
Let me lean on Thy spirit for all I must face.
I can accomplish all, when filled with Thy grace."

Jesus tries again to wake His dear friends,
upset that they have no comfort to lend.
"What! Can ye not watch with me one hour?"
Pray ye be not tempted through Satan's power!"

Alone yet again, once more He will pray.
He will not be tempted His duty to sway.
Still troubled, He wrestles with what must be done.
Yet He vows to be a loyal, faithful Son.

Oh where are the multitudes that came,
to hear Him speak and praise His name?
Where are all the ones He so gently healed?
Does anyone care if His blood will spill?

Into His heart now, the sorrow is locked.
He gives His last plea there beside the rock.
"Again, dear Father of Thee I will ask
that Thy will be done, I can face this task.

I know Thou art with me, bring it all on.
Soon I will join You at Our kingdom's throne.
As He prays this one last final prayer,
from ether plains comes the angels' care.

Through the whisper of night the angels sing.
Unheard by mortals, their tribute they bring.
The comfort Christ sought, His Father now sends.
One last time, Jesus wakes His sleeping friends.

Concerned at last, they rise to their feet
as a commotion is coming form the Garden deep.
His disciple was coming, Jesus to betray.
For thirty pieces of silver Judas had swayed.

By a kiss on the cheek, he gave them our Lord,
and Peter, in the crowd swiftly used his sword.
Still our Savior would no resistance do,
for He knew that the scriptures must come true.

Gently He reach out and healed the ear
that had been cut off through anger and fear.
The disciples, afraid, how quickly they fled.
Only Peter now followed in Jesus stead.

In the dark of early morning light,
he would sneak and follow, for it was not right.
This treatment the Master did not deserve!
He would follow along, listen and observe.

Perhaps it was all some silly mistake.
Though frightened, he'd see what was at stake.
Surely all that Jesus said would come
was not for the Christ, the Father's Son!

...Then saith Jesus unto them; All ye shall be offended because of Me this night: for it is written, I will smite the shepherd, and the sheep of the flock shall be scattered abroad. But after I am risen again, I will go before you into Galilee. Peter answered and said unto Him, "Though all men shall be offended because of Thee, yet will I never be offended." Jesus said unto him, "Verily I say unto thee, That this night, before the cock crow, thou shalt deny me thrice." Peter said unto Him, "Though I should die with Thee, yet will I not deny thee. Likewise also said all the disciples....Matthew 26: 31 - 35 KJV

Prediction's Truth, Denial's Cost

All the disciples of Christ from Gethsemane had fled.
They feared the soldiers, and the cost that Christ said
would need to be paid to stop evil's hold.
Where was their courage, their strength so bold?

Just as Peter had promised His Lord he would do,
he meant to stay faithful, and ever true.
Peter understood not what was yet to be,
or the heartbreaking horrors he soon would see.

His Master was captured, what could one man do?
Yet he'd promised Jesus he would stay true.
He would just follow, see what would be.
He would not turn as the others and flee!

He must be careful or they'd capture him too.
Then he might face judgment, or worse, death's due.
So carefully he lingered by the campfire's light,
to see just what cost Christ would pay for right.

Thus as a maiden by the campfire's light,

asked Peter if he followed Jesus that night;
just as Jesus had once said he would,
Peter denied his Lord as fast as he could.

Yet another maiden asked the same thing again.
Still his faith faltered, Peter's fear was fanned.
When thrice he was asked if he knew the Lord,
Peter got so angry that he even swore!

The cock had yet to crow just twice,
when Christ was denied, not once, but thrice!
When Peter heard that second crow of the cock,
he hung down his head in horror and shock.

How could he have done as His Lord had spoken?
He cast down his eyes, for his heart was broken.
Now in tears Peter turned, to flee like the rest.
The cost of betrayal lay on Jesus' breast.

Only Christ's great love could conquer such pain,
such humiliation, ridicule, and disdain.
Jesus knew the path He had vowed to take.
Knew alone He must carry this cost so great.

Knew His Father's face would need turn away,
as His Son met with death through evil's great sway.
All alone, Christ would face the death of the cross
and Satan would dance at the thought of Christ's loss.

Satan too soon would celebrate Jesus' demise.
This was God's own plan, soon He'd hold the prize.
Quietly and bravely, both faced the Son's doom.
Knowing victory would come after death's dark gloom.

Joy again would come with the morning's light

as the cost of victory regained it's might.
Christ would arise above death's sting,
to live forever, as our Lord and King.

Just as Jesus arose to live once more,
we too shall rise, live forevermore.
Eternity will be ours, if we choose to believe,
to repent our sins and forgiveness receive.

What cost have we? None it's all been paid,
by the Shepherd who came with love to our aid.
O death where thy victory, thy bitter sting,
Now forever with the angels we too can sing!

Jesus Christ is our Lord, forever to be.
His love paid the price, we have been set free.
Will you accept this gift, so grand and rare?
Or will the devil's loss become the path you share?

The choice is yours, what will you believe?
Is it victory or loss that you will receive?
I am praying for you, Jesus asked me to.
Without ceasing, I pray for your victory too.

Will you betray Him again today.
Or by love's sweet light will your heart sway?
The truth of His sacrifice hangs in the air.
What cost denial? Why pay that share?

Freedom from sin? Oh that cost is paid.
In the gloom of grave that price was laid.
Jesus cancelled that cost, arose from the dead.
Now in His acceptance, we've no cost to dread.

Prediction's truth, denial's cost

Has been set free, and the devil has lost.
Oh sweet victory, so glad, so free,
How thankful am I, the Lord let it be.

...Those who had arrested Jesus took Him to Caiaphas, the high priest, where the teachers of the law and the elders had assembled... The chief priest and the whole Sanhedrin were looking for false evidence against Jesus so that they could put Him to death. But they did not find any, though many false witnesses came forward....Then the high priest tore his clothes and said, "He has spoken blasphemy! Why do we need any more witnesses? Look, now you have heard the blasphemy....Then they spit in His face and struck Him with their fists. Others slapped Him...Matthew 26: 57, 59, 65 & 67 NIV...Pilate called together the chief priests, the rulers and the people, and said to them, "You have brought me this man as one who was inciting the people to rebellion. I have examined Him in your presence and have found no basis for your charges against Him...Therefore, I will punish Him and then release Him."...With one voice they cried out, "Away with this man! Release Barabbas to us!"...Luke 23: 13, 14, 16, & 18...While Pilate was sitting on the judge's seat, his wife sent him this message: "Don't have anything to do with that innocent man, for I have suffered a great deal today in a dream because of Him."... When Pilate saw that he was getting nowhere, but that instead an uproar was starting, he took water and washed his hands in front of the crowd. "I am innocent of this man's blood." he said. "It is your responsibility!"...Matthew 27: 19 & 24 NIV...Wanting to release Jesus, Pilate appealed to them again. But they kept shouting," Crucify Him! Crucify Him!"...So Pilate decided to grant their demand. He released the man who had been thrown into prison for insurrection and murder, the one they asked for, and surrendered Jesus to their will...Luke 23: 20, & 23, NIV...

Jesus Stood On Trial

Judean Scribes and Pharisees, the Sadducees as well,
wanted Jesus punished, for in their hearts did swell:
envy, fear and bitterness; they'd seen the people turned
away from them, unto the Christ; oh how their hatred burned!

In secret, they insisted all Christ's teachings be denied.
So they captured Him by midnight's light, and took Him to be tried.
The took Him first to Caiphas, high priest among their peers.
They felt they had the right, because His teachings they did fear.

Many testified against Him but their words did not agree,
because the ones who testified told lies of all degree.
When finally Christ admitted to the answer that they sought,
Caiphas tore his clothes into, so much was he distraught.

It was blasphemy He spoke, they all agreed on that.
He should die, they raised their fists, and in his face they spat.
They bound His hands and had Him sent to the governor of the land.
They wanted Jesus crucified, but not by their own hand.

Thus He stood before the governor to account for His good deeds,
but Pontius Pilate found no fault, he thought Christ should be freed.
The elders, Jews and scribes there knew no justice on their part.
They demanded He be punished, for envy ruled their hearts.

The crowd was soon persuaded to seek the crucifixion price,
and Pontius Pilate would not stand against such strong advice.
Instead he quickly gave unto his soldiers this decree:
"Have Him lashed upon His back until the blood flows free."

He thought that such an action might appease the angry crowd.
Maybe pity would be felt, enough to calm their cries so loud.
The whip was swiftly brought out and the lashes harshly laid!
Sharply! Deeply! Across His back, but no whimper there was made.

The skin was torn, drenched in His blood, His strength began to languor,
yet meek and mild the Christ remained and showed to them no anger.
Then, they took a crow of thorns, dug it deeply in His brow.
They slapped and spit, ridiculed His name, then showed Him to the crowd.

Pilate asked if such a punishment would satisfy the people's plight.
Instead the crowd grew louder still, as if thirsty for a fight.
There was a custom with the Jews upon Passover Day.
Rome would free one prisoner, Pilate hoped the crowd to sway.

He wanted Christ to be freed, even his own wife had fears.
She'd dreamed Jesus was too good to meet His judgment here.
She had asked her husband, "Leave this innocent man alone."
Yet Pilate could not do this, to the crowd he must atone.

Pilate gave them one last chance, "This one day you may choose,
which prisoner I will release, which prisoner will lose.
Shall I free Barabbas, well- known murderer and thief,
or Jesus Christ, a simple man, who has not caused such grief?"

Too quick the multitude replied in anger and dismay,
showing no compassion for the Christ now on display.
Crucify Him! Crucify Him" was their battle cry!
Pilate shrugged his shoulders, he really cared not how or why.

He just aimed to keep the peace with all these priests so odd.
He had no faith or justice, believed not in their God.
"Give them what they ask," he said with nonchalant an air,
and picking up a towel, washed his hands of the affair.

Thus upon Christ's shoulders, the rugged cross was placed.
Though He was accused unjustly, with death He now was faced.
Weak from being beaten, struggling with the heavy cross,
with grace He struggled up the hill, to Calvary and it's loss.

For each of us, His love flowed deep, He'd pay the price for all,
even though He knew not all would heed His loving call.
If one be saved, He'd gladly lay His own life freely down.
He knew His Father waited, with eternity's golden crown.

The trial now was over and the die would soon be cast,
as the hope of man's salvation for all eternity would last.
More pain and agony still would come, He'd bear it all with grace.
He'd stay true to His Father's plan, throw love in hatred's face.

Death would not be the victor, evil would not rule God's King.
When the right time came, then God would send Him back to reign.
The victory was not His to claim, but His Father's up above.
The victory was for man-kind too, so great for us their love.

...And when they were come unto a place called Golgotha, that is to say, a place of a skull, They gave Him vinegar to drink mingled with gall: and when He had tasted thereof He would not drink. And they crucified Him, and parted His garments, casting lots: that it might be fulfilled which was spoken by the prophet, "They parted My garments among them, and upon My vesture did they cast lots."... Then were there two thieves crucified with Him, one on the right hand, and another on the left. And they that passed by reviled Him, wagging their heads..."He trusted in God; let Him deliver Him now, if He will have Him: for He said, I am the Son of God."...And about the ninth hour Jesus cried with a loud voice, saying, "Eli, Eli, Lamasabachthani? That is to say, My God, My God, why hast Thou forsaken Me?"...Matthew 27: 33 – 35, 38, 39, 43, & 46 KJV...When Jesus therefore saw His mother, and the disciple standing by, whom He loved, He saith unto His mother, "Woman, behold thy son!" Then saith He to the disciple, "Behold thy mother!" And from that hour that disciple took her unto his own home.
    ...John 19: 26 & 27 KJV...And the sun was darkened, and the veil of the temple was rent in the midst. And when Jesus had cried with a loud voice, He said, "Father, into Thy hands I commend My spirit;" and having said thus, He gave up the ghost.
    ...Luke 24: 45 & 46 KJV

Behold The Cross

Behold the cross! Symbol of greatest sacrifice.
For our daily sins, Jesus paid the highest price.
Stop and take a moment, be still, visit there with me.
Come see, come feel, come hear with me, our Savior's agony.

Already He's been beaten until the blood flows free.
Watching from the sidelines, feel His mother's agony?
Watch as Jesus stumbles beneath the weight of heavy cross.
Feel His knees go limp, as most of His strength is lost?

Gaze upon the dried up blood still caked upon His face,
from the thorny crown that upon His brow was placed.
Feel the sharpening pain as the nails are hammered deep,
first into His hands and then into His feet?

Hear the ridicule that the people at Him slang?
See the wicked men between which He was hanged?
When He said, "I thirst," it was not water that they dipped.
Taste the vinegar and gall that they lifted to His lips?

Feel the swollen throat through which no drink was passed?
See His finest garment, upon which lots were cast?
Hear the lingering echoes that weigh heavy in the air
of how our Savior suffered for long hours hanging there?

Feel the love He gives, as He leaves His weeping mother
gently in the care of His most beloved brother?
Hear His sweet compassion, as He asks they be forgiven?
Feel the empty loneliness, hear Him cry out to God in heaven?

Hear His sweet surrender as into His Father's hands
He commits His precious spirit for all man-kind to stand?
See the stormy darkness as the curtain's torn into?
Feel the helplessness, His followers know not what to do?

Even after death, feel the spear pierced in His side?
Hanging on the cross alone, so painfully He died.
Feel the weight of cost, upon the shoulders of His soul?
See His sacrifice, a gift of love that was so bold?

In your mind, your heart, see our Savior hanging there?
Listen! Look and feel it! With our Master let us share.
What if Jesus hadn't paid the price for freedom's gain?
Never then would we from death be risen once again.

Were we now this moment, asked to pay that heavy price,
not for ourselves but others, would we make that sacrifice?
Would our love, our courage, our strength be ever strong?
Do we care enough when we remember what went on?

Is not the debt He paid for us most worthy to recall?
Can we simply turn our backs, forget His love for all?
Should we not live as He did, caring for one another?
Can we not show compassion for our sisters and our brothers?

Behold the cross! Symbol of greatest sacrifice!
For our daily sins, Jesus paid the highest price.
Lord, may I oft remember, all the love You have for me!
May I never Lord forget the price you paid to set us free..

May I oft behold the memory, of that rugged cross so dear.
May I take time to be grateful of Your love so ever near.
Behold the cross! Symbol of greatest sacrifice!
How joyfully I claim it! No other love could dare suffice!

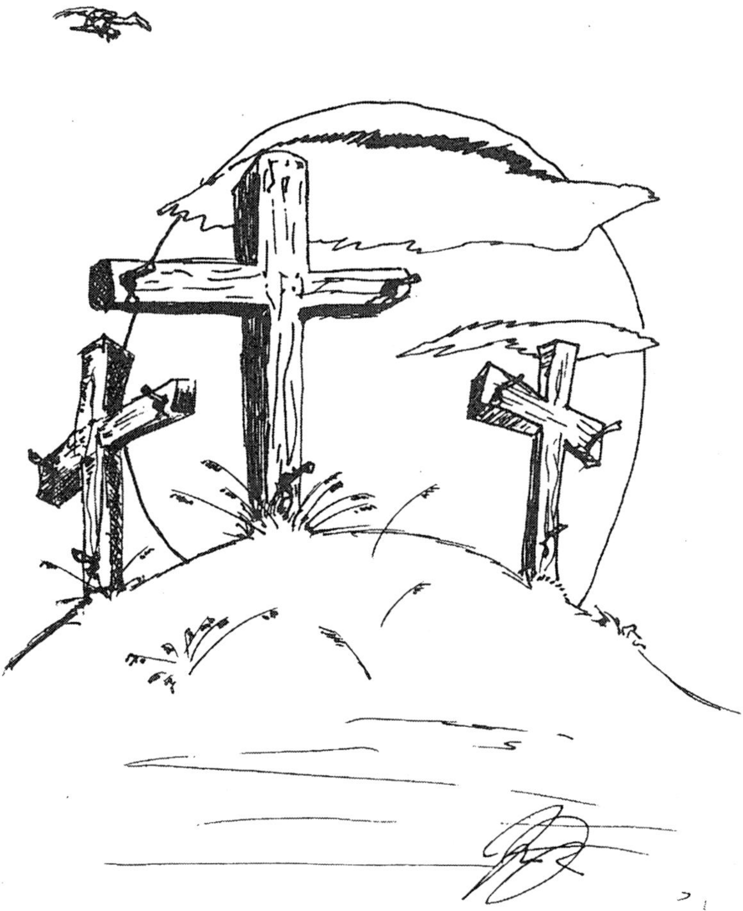

...Jesus said to them, "The time has come for the Son of Man to receive His glory. I tell you the truth, a grain of wheat must fall to the ground and die to make many seeds. But if it never dies, it remains only a single seed...Whoever serves Me must follow Me. Then my servant will be with Me everywhere I am. My Father will honor anyone who serves me. Now I am very troubled. Should I say, "Father, save Me from this time? No, I came to this time so I could suffer. Father, bring glory to Your name!" Then a voice came from heaven, "I have brought glory to it and I will do it again."...John 12: 23, 24, 26 – 28 NIV

What Price Glory?

Salvation carried cost so great, mere man could not atone.
That price would be paid by the Savior and the Father, both alone.
Jesus suffered agony, do you think that God did not?
While watching as the father of all evil laid his plot?

Christ stood firm throughout the ridicule and beatings He would bear.
Through hammered nails in hands and feet, received because He cared.
For hours He hung dying upon Calvary's weighted cross,
accepting with forgiving grace, the ones He knew were lost.

Jesus knew and He accepted the price that He must pay.
The Father knew too with Him, that there would come the day,
that He must set aside His power, His deep love for His Son.
Must turn His back upon the agony of sacrifice begun.

Above the Garden of Gethsemane, He listened to Christ's prayers.
Then sent His angels to Christ with His comfort, strength and care.
Yet after that dark midnight of Mount Olive's deep distress,
the Father turned His back, His love He needed to repress.

The sights, the sounds, the agony and pain that Jesus bore?
The Father must ignore them all, His kingdom to restore.

He loved the Son with all His heart, but this was the chosen hour,
to show the world that in His hands lay grace of highest power.

The Father could have stopped it all, so too could His precious Son.
Yet if either changed a single thing, their plan would be undone.
Each knew the cost, each vowed to stay, their spirits were combined.
The fate of all man-kind would from this moment be entwined.

This was the magnitude of cost to bring the world aright.
To keep God's children in His will, exchange all wrongs for right.
Forgiveness through the Son would bring acceptance to our Lord.
This was the price required to keep man safe forevermore.

Do you think that it was easy for the Father as He watched?
Why let Jesus suffer so? He carried not sin's darkened blotch.
Could you, could I bear anything to hurt our hearts this much?
Greater strength cannot be found to meet such loving touch.

Could you turn away, ignore the agony and strife.
Would you beg release for Him, offer instead your life?
This is what He did for you, for me, for all of man.
This is where the Father and the Son joined in their stand.

Such pain is not so fleeting, God never meant for it to be.
He took this stand for you and I, for all eternity,
to save His children from the dark of sin's most evil reign.
Yet He vowed His Son would soon be glorified again.

This time the name of Jesus would rise above all names supreme.
Christ would wear God's golden crown, Christ would reign as King.
He brought glory to the Father everyday He walked this earth.
The Father gives it back to Him, and it bears the greatest worth.

Jehovah is the God of man, believe He sent His Son!
Without believe, God turns away, once life on earth is done.

Glorify the Father, through the Son sent to reclaim
all the Father's children, give glad praise unto His name.
The Father, Son and Holy Ghost, deserve the highest praise
for all that has been given us, in His love we can graze.
What price glory? Can't you see? The price was always to be paid
through hearts of unconditional love, on their shoulders love was laid.

Yes too, the cost was carried by the One Most High of all.
While His Son did the dying, He heeded not temptation's call.
Satan would have loved it, if either one of them caved in.
The devil cannot understand such deep love from within.

It bears repeating over, until the truth is realized.
There is no other love so true, nor any greater prize.
The cost of glory was so high, how grateful we should be,
that Jesus' unconditional love came to us all for free.

Hallelujah! His the Glory! Hallelujah, and Amen!
Laud and honor should be given, to our Savior, Christ our friend.
Hallelujah! His the Glory! To Jehovah our dear Lord.
Laud and honor be Thy footrest, today, and forevermore.

There is now therefore no condemnation to them that are in Christ Jesus, who walk not according to the flesh, but according to Spirit.

And after this, Joseph of Arimathaea, being a disciple of Jesus, but secretly for fear of the Jews, besought Pilate that he might take away the body of Jesus. And there came Nicodemus, which at the first came to Jesus by night, and brought a mixture of myrrh and aloes, about an hundred pound weight. Then took they the body of Jesus, and wound it in linen clothes with the spices, as the manner of the Jews is to bury....John 19: 38, 39 KJV...Now the next day, that followed the day of the preparation, the chief priests and Pharisees came together unto Pilate...Command therefore that the sepulcher be made sure until the third day, lest His disciples come by night, and steal Him away, and say unto the people, He is risen from the dead: so the last error shall be worse than the first. So they went and made the sepulcher sure, sealing the stone, and setting a watch....Matthew 28: 62, 64, 66 KJV

Paying Tribute

Through all that Jesus suffered to wash away our sins,
He walked a very lonely path, deserted by His friends.
Only one small handful of people loved Him still,
even though they knew not just why His blood was spilled.

Where before they had been faithful, they now were lost, confused.
They felt abandoned, frightened, would they be next abused?
Came one of them to offer a tomb where Christ could lay.
While others sought to place a guard, for they had heard Him say:
"In just three days this temple that you refuse to cherish
shall be torn down and built again; but those who doubt will perish!
For I shall be the only hope throughout the generations.
All shall bow and praise My name, each one from all the nations.

Those who heed the Shepherd's voice, My precious lambs shall be.
I'll reunite them with our Father, but this wonder you'll not see.
Only those who will accept on faith the Father's Son
will rise to share His glory when their life on earth is done.

I am the Shepherd they will seek, My lambs will heed my call.
Salvation I am offering, through faith, to each and all."
Afraid these words might be believed, a guard would leave no room
for faithful followers to sneak around and steal Christ from His tomb.

Thus the guard was set to watch, just as the Scribes had asked.
To watch from dusk 'til dawn three days; this was their only task.
Jealous greed and anarchy, no tribute there would bring.
Why should Christ be honored, they felt He was no King.

The small group that still loved Him, in spite of fear and doubt,
would prepare for Him a burial worthy of their friend devout.
Passover duties must be met, but immediately thereafter,
they would visit at the tomb, tribute to bring the Master.

This was all that they had left, was all that they could do,
the only way to honor Him, to show their love was true.
Grief and fear might rule the dark, as their Master now lay dead.
But joy comes in the morning, soon, they'd have naught to dread.

...And behold, there was a great earthquake: for the angel of the Lord descended from heaven, and came and rolled back the stone from the door, and sat upon it...And for fear of him, the keepers did shake, and became as dead men...And when they were assembled with the elders, and had taken council, they gave large money unto the soldiers, Saying, "Say ye, His disciples came by night, and stole Him away while we slept."...So they took the money, and did as they were taught: and this saying is commonly reported among the Jews until this day...Matthew 28: 2, 4, 12 & 15 KJV...On the first day of the week, very early in the morning, the women took the spices they had prepared and went to the tomb. They found the stone rolled away from the tomb, but when they entered, they did not find the body of the Lord Jesus....."Why do you look for the living among the dead? He is not here; he has risen!...When they came back from the tomb, they told all these things to the eleven and to all the others...Luke 24: 1-3, 5, & 9 NIV

Joy Comes In The Morning

After Jesus suffered and died on Calvary's cross,
His followers hid in trembling fear, all they could see was loss.
On that first Sunday morning, three days after He was dead,
came some women to His grave, hearts filled with fear and dread.
They planned to show Him honor with spices and perfume,
but at His place of rest that morn, He lay not in the tomb.
What was this? Where could He be? His body had been taken!
The wrappings He'd been buried in laid empty and forsaken!

An angel sat inside the tomb, asked Mary Magdalene,
"Why seek Him here? He told you, He would once again be seen."
The women were bewildered and fled in fear and haste.
Seeing there a gardener, Magdalene asked where Christ was placed?
"Mary", Jesus softly spoke, "Do you not know that it is I?"
She recognized her Master, and fell down at His side.
When she would have reached out, to touch the Master's feet,
He warned her not to do so for His task was not complete.

To the Father He'd not risen yet, she must now do as bidden.
She must go and tell the others, let not the news be hidden.
Jesus Christ now lived again, and He would see them there.
She must have been excited, running with her news to share.
O that we might have that passion, as we greet today the lost.
O that we rejoice in telling how our Savior paid the cost.
Only those who come to God through Jesus Christ the Son
will gain eternal life with Him, then Satan will be done.

As long as word is spread of all that Jesus came to do,
the gift of sweet eternity can be for all believers true.
Let the news still spread like wildfire, throughout all time and space,
of the joy that came one morning through the loving Savior's grace.
His Light has conquered darkness, our joy can stay complete,
as long as we are willing to lay our hearts at Jesus' feet.
Confess our sins and claim Him as our own Savior and Lord,
then we shall know such love and peace as never known before.

Why can't you believe all this? Why doubt the way they did?
Listen to His whispers. In your heart hear His sweet bid.
He longs so much to be found, how can you not hear?
Seek Him now I beg you, call for His love to come so near.
And if you have already, then aren't you glad the choice you made?
Helping others who don't know Him yet, accept His plan now laid?
Rejoice! Rejoice! O Christians, for we have much to sing about!
Much to show all non-believers of His precious love devout.

Though many still will scoff at us, just as they did back then,
We have His strength behind us, and that strength never will end.
We must keep right on telling, as long as we shall breathe,
that all can live in peace and joy, if His love they'll receive.
Joy came on Sunday morning, three days after He had died.
That joy will last forever, for His blood has been applied.
Give tribute now all Christians, to our Savior, Master, King.
Forever with our voices let His sweet praise boldly ring!

...When Jesus rose early on the first day of the week, He appeared first to Mary Magdalene, out of whom He had driven seven demons. She went and told those who had been with Him and who were mourning and weeping. When they heard that Jesus was alive and that she had seen Him, they did not believe it...Afterward Jesus appeared in a different form to two of them while they were walking in the country. These returned and reported it to the rest; but they did not believe them either...Mark: 16: 9 – 13 KJV

O Ye Of Little Faith

Swiftly from the tomb of Christ, Mary ran to tell
how the Master lived again, how joy in her did swell.
"His tomb, no longer covered, now is empty as can be!
An angel sat inside and said, "He's gone, come look and see."

"Shocked at first I wondered where His body had been taken.
Then I thought I saw a gardener, but He said I was mistaken."
"Mary, don't you recognize me? Go and tell them I have risen.
How through my resurrection new life they can be given.

I go now to My Father, but there is much they'll need to do.
I will meet them as I said, they must believe that's true."
"I left with haste to come and tell you, just as I was told.
You must believe me, it's all true, although it sounds so bold!"

The disciples though did not believe, it simply could not be!
She kept insisting, and others too, still they just would not see.
Two others ran to check the tomb, in disbelief they thought to find,
Mary surely was not right, in grief she'd lost her mind.

Though they found no body in the tomb where He'd been laid,
understanding did not come, they rushed back still afraid.
Could He rise up from the dead? Other wonders they had seen,
but to believe in such as this, to them seem quite obscene!

As they stood there pondering, 'lo in their midst appeared,
Jesus Christ their risen Lord, to conquer all they feared.
"Why are you troubled, why do you doubt? I told you this would be.
Look and see, touch these my scars. It is I, can't you see?"

The disciples now would dare believe, they saw with their own eyes,
but Jesus quickly told them faith without sight was the prize.
Thomas was not with them, that first time Jesus came.
He too swore he would not believe until he'd seen the same.

How sweet that our salvation rests not in the minds of man.
How precious that the heart receives what is not held by hand.
Thank you Lord, that we receive much more than can be seen.
Thank you that your presence is for all who are redeemed.

For all who will receive through faith, the promises Christ made.
Salvation is the prize received, through Christ the price was paid.
His sacrifice upon that cross, His resurrection soon to follow,
gave to each who would believe His grace for all our sorrow.

No more do we live in fear of Satan's great temptations.
Now we live in hope and joy, we have God's sweet salvation.
The joy that came that morning, will now forever reign
in the hearts of those believing that Jesus lives again.

Christ the victor evermore, has paid the price for all,
and Satan can not stand against the Master's loving call.
Oh ye of little faith step forth, come boldly to God's Light.
Accept the chosen Lamb of God, accept His strength and might.

Through the resurrection of God's Sacrificial Lamb,
we all are reconciled through grace with God, the great I AM.
Thanks be to our Father, for this gift so sweet and rare.
Thanks be to our Savior for the love He laid down there.

Hallelujahs rise forever, all laud and honor raise.
Jesus Christ the Son of God is worthy of all praise.
The Father raises high the name of Christ, His Chosen One,
above all other names on earth, gives power to His Son.

From the right hand of God's throne, all judgment be received.
Sing praise unto the Three in One, all who will dare believe.
Yes joy comes in the morning, in the day and in the night,
for all who choose to trust in Him, our Savior, Lord, and Light!

...So the disciples told him, "We have seen the Lord!" But he said to them, "Unless I see the nail marks in His hands, and put my finger where the nails were, and put my hand into His side, I will not believe it." A week later His disciples were in the house again, and Thomas was with them. Though the doors were locked, Jesus came and stood among them and said, "Peace be with you!" Then He said to Thomas, "Put your finger here; see My hands. Reach out your hand and put it into my side. Stop doubting and believe!"...Then Jesus told him, "Because you have seen me, you have believed; blessed are those who have not seen and yet have believed." John 20: 25 – 27, & 29

On Faith Alone

Came to us a Savior, lowly in a stable born,
that would become Redeemer to the lost, broken, forlorn.
He'd touch the hearts of all He met, in one way or another.
Some would call Him enemy, while others called Him brother.

Some would proclaim Him Lord and King, still others would not dare.
Some would nail Him to a cross, some watch in deep despair.
Some would say He rose again, a victory to proclaim!
Others dared not to believe, unless they saw the same.

Faith is the substance of things not seen, cannot be held by hand.
Yet it's power can rise and conquer temptations strongest stand.
Just look at all the power the apostle's realized!
Once they truly understood the resurrection prize.

They too doubted when Christ died, it simply could not be!
Especially Thomas, who demanded, "He must touch and see!
To place his hands within the scars which now the Savior wore
was the only way that he'd trust in what his friends now swore.

He felt that without proof of eye, or proof of scar on hand,
Christ could not rise up from the dead to save His fellowman.
Once the Christ appeared again, let Thomas see and touch,
Christ said belief on faith alone is what would mean so much.

Then to His apostles, a commission soon was given:
they were to pass His message on, tell others He was risen.
See how all was sacrificed, to send the gospel out?
Not just by Christ alone, but His apostles firm and stout.

They too were persecuted for their teaching of the cross.
From then on each one diligently reached out to all the lost.
Once convicted of their faith, they honored Jesus' call.
They spent the rest of their own lives telling the news to all.

Thus His life would change so much, the lives of all who heard,
whether or not they'd dare believe, in the spreading of His word.
Now here we stand in present day, and still man-kind's not sure.
Dare we believe on faith alone, that this man's love was pure?

Some even claim He never lived, still search for proof to see.
They need to touch before they'll give acceptance of His seed.
Faith is not so tangible, it can't be bought or sold.
It can't be bargained, can't be denied; it's worth much more than gold.

Jesus said, "Blessed are those who will believe it's so,
without seeing or touching , to help their weak faith grow.
Loving faith from heart sincere, means so much more to Me
Than faithless love that's only found in what you touch or see.

Stand fast upon your faith alone, and live the Father's will.
It's for this unseen faith that I allowed my blood to spill.
I believed in each of you, prayed for you even then,
and throughout time, I will remain, my love shall know no end."

Jesus' resurrection can bring sweet joy and hope to all,
as long as each is willing to receive the Master's call.
Many today will not believe, they let their peers decide.
Better to fit within this world, than in Christ to abide.

Confession of our sinful deeds, will bring a sweet release
from all the doubts and fears we have and bring us grace and peace.
Word must spread throughout the world, the price our Jesus paid.
Sin has been conquered through His grace, God's will should be obeyed.

Come judgment day each life will claim the reward that is its due.
I pray on faith you will believe, pass on His message true.
Stand firm, stand fast, against the storms of Satan's tricky ways.
He will find your weakest links and on those he will prey.

He'll use our fears and weaknesses just as he did back then;
just the way he preyed on Christ's disciples, and His friends.
Though only for a little while, they too let doubts and fears
lead them to forget the promises He made so very clear.

We too have our weaknesses, our fears, our trials and doubts.
Yet if we seek His power, we can turn them all about.
Jesus is the lighthouse that leads you through the devil's maze.
Cling firmly, always to His love, on His strength you can graze.

Be thou not discouraged, but in all things give Him praise.
He has already shown how much His faith in each is raised.
He will not forsake or leave you hopeless in the night.
He has already fought the war, brought darkness into light.

He turned the tide of His believers, once they came to realize:
even death holds not His light. Believe in Him, our prize.
Don't let the devil shake your faith, cause doubt within your mind.
He'll try every trick he knows, to keep you in his bind.

We need only make our choice, believe Christ lives today.
Let your heart accept His truth, and do not doubt His way.
Let faith stand firm in Jesus, and the promises He's made.
Build upon that faith each day, the foundation has been laid.

When that tempter shakes and roars, Christ's power you can claim.
Faith overcomes those fears and doubts if you trust in His name.
Our Redeemer lives today, tomorrow and forever.
Let faith in Christ become your life's most precious, true endeavor.

"Believe in Me," the Master said, "Don't worry fret or doubt."
I have overcome the world, in you My faith is stout.
I believe with all my heart in who you can become.
Won't you accept who I must be: the Father's only Son?

I gave My life to prove My love, what more child, can I do?
The Father sent Me this to do, because His love is true.
Do not wonder how or why, be bold, be brave, be strong!
All these gifts the Spirit gives, must come through faith alone!

Come walk forever in My light, and share My news with all.
For this purpose I was sent, come heed the Father's call.
You decide, the Father wants the choice to be your own.
Let love choose, your heart will be forever filled with song.

...After His suffering, He showed Himself to these men and gave many convincing proofs that He was alive. He appeared to them over a period of forty days and spoke about the kingdom of God...Acts 2:3 NIV

Appearance By The Sea

Some disciples came together to go fishing in the sea.
There they were joined by Jesus, but knew not that it was He.
Christ asked of His disciples, "Have ye any meat?"
But after fishing through the night, no fish they'd caught to eat.

He told them then to cast their net to the right side of the ship,
and though the men were doubtful, again their net they dipped.
Then 'lo before their very eyes, the net was quickly full.
Now so many fish they caught, the net was hard to pull.

Then the beloved disciple said to Peter, "It is the Lord."
And Peter gave to Christ his coat, for no clothes Jesus wore.
When the ships had come to land, Jesus joined the men to dine,
and counting His appearances, this now was the third time.

Once more the Lord spoke to them of things they'd need to know
before He'd finally leave them and to His Father go.
One time when Jesus met with them, they all asked of the Lord,
"Master is this now the time that Israel is to be restored?"

Jesus then rebuked them, "It's not your place or mine to know,
the time the Father chooses, His authority to show.
Yet do not leave Jerusalem, for His spirit He will send,
and ye shall be My witnesses of light the dark to rend.

After He had said this, they saw Him lifted in a cloud,
and then two men appeared to them, their clothes as a white shroud.

"Men of Galilee, why stand ye there, still looking to the sky?
The Jesus you saw lifted up will come back by and by.

From the clouds He will descend and all will see 'tis so.
But only those who lived for Him will reap rewards they sowed.
The ones too busy, who cared not, who turned their backs to Him
will face eternal judgment for their lack of faith so dim.

What will be your judgment friend, we each must face it all.
I pray you lived your life in faith, on Jesus Christ to call.
Then sweet will be all you'll receive, eternity to claim.
And all will live forever to rejoice in His sweet name.

...Blessed is he that readeth, and they that hear the words of this prophecy, and keep those things which are written therein: the time is at hand...Behold He cometh with clouds; and every eye shall see Him, and they also which pierced Him: and all kindreds of the earth shall wail because of Him. Even so, Amen...And when I saw Him, I fell at His feet as dead. And He laid His right hand upon me, saying unto me, "Fear not; I am the first and the last: I am He that liveth, and was dead; and, behold, I am alive forevermore, Amen; and have the keys of hell and of death. Write the things which thou has seen, and the things which are, and the things which shall be hereafter;... Revelation 1: 3, 7,

17 – 19KJV...For the great day of His wrath is come; and who shall be able to stand?
...Revelation 6: 17 KJV...

Revelation's Promise

Revelation tells how John saw other prophecies would come.
How in the clouds the Christ would come, as King, as Father's Son.

How trials and tribulations before time began were sealed.
How those who would reject the Christ, faced horrible ordeals.

Christ would be the only One with worth to read the scrolls.
There upon the throne He sat, 'twas planned from times of old.

Here written are just part of all that John saw in this dream.
Horrors, wonders, death and fear as man could never scheme.

Seven seals then would be broken, and after all of that came true,
seven angels with seven trumpets prepared to sound their hue.

Hail and fire came, mixed with blood, one-third of earth lay burned.
A mountain fell into the sea, ships and sea life lay dead, upturned.

Fresh waters turned so bitter, there was none left fit to drink.
The sun, the moon, the stars were struck, in dark one-third would sink.

Opened was the great Abyss, smoke rose like a mighty furnace.
And locusts fed upon all those whom God's mark did not possess.

Those were the days that man cried out in such pain and miseries,
"Let us die!" but God would not, for they had done such evil deeds.

Two hundred million troops came down, to slaughter more untrue.
Yet still theses plagues turned not around the evil men would do.

John was told to eat the angel's scroll, to prophesy as well,
Of many peoples, nations, kings, so much had John to tell.

Two others two would prophesy, as told to by the Lord.
They could not be stuck down by man or evil's sharpest sword.

If one should try to harm them, before their time was due,
They had the power to stop the rain, use plagues on people too.

A woman and a dragon appeared in heaven to be seen.
His desire was her destruction, but her protection was too keen.

Enraged the dragon turned his wrath on the offspring of her womb.
A beast came from the sea, allied with evil, seeking doom.

God needed to be slandered, they made war against God's saints.
With trickery and cruelty, they fooled the world with such disdain.

Another beast came from the earth, with great, miracles and signs.
Forcing all to take his mark or face death of his designs.

Off with all heads of those who would not worship as he said.
Deceiving all the world, saying that there was naught to dread.

Still there would be salvation, for the ones who'd come to Christ,
but woe be unto all of those who would reject His sacrifice.

Too was heard the song of heaven, only chosen ones could sing.
One hundred forty-four were offered as first fruits of God's King.

An angel flew in mid-air, proclaiming gospel as He went.
"Fear God and give Him glory, for comes His time of swift judgment."

Other angels followed. Warned how evil soon would fall.
Torment for them would never end, they refused to heed God's call.

A sickle would be brought out, all evil man cut down.
Before all this could happen, much more woe would be unbound.

Seven more angels carried to the earth seven more plagues.
These would be the last that upon the earth was laid.

These plagues angels carried in seven bowls to be poured out.
First came painful sores for those who wore the beast's mark all about.

The second bowl turned seas to blood, and all sea life then died.
The forth bowl, burning sun to scorch, nowhere could man-kind hide.

The fifth bowl brought such darkness to the kingdom of the beast.
Men gnawed their tongues in agony, yet still hungered for his feast.

The sixth bowl dried Euphrates, preparing way for eastern kings.
Still one more bowl to be poured out, more grief and pain to bring.

The three spirits of the demons showed more miracles and signs.
Soon all would join in one great battle to crush out the Lord's designs.

For the Father's Lamb, a marriage supper was arranged.
A feast as never seen before, great joy there interchanged.

The faithful ones would dine with Him, all equal, great or small.
For all are special to the Lamb, the heeding the Master's call.

The three evil spirits captured, thrown into the deep Abyss.
A thousand years of peaceful reign, with joy and sweetest bliss.

Thus fulfilled the promise made to Israel long ago.
The earth would be their holy land, they'd need no other place to go.

Just one remnant of all Israel, just the ones who stayed so true.
Harps would sing the song of Moses, and the song of Christ, His due.

Armageddon was still yet to come, evil would try for one last war.
The Lord would let the evil rise to fight, God would win the final score.

The anti-Christ would use his all, but would meet final defeat.
Prophecies foretold it, all in time would be complete.

Great trials and tribulations, the faithful had to overcome,
But evil would at last lose out, the victor: Christ, God's Son.

Into the great eternal lake of fire, all evil then be thrown.
Along with all its followers, too late the truth be known.

God's judgment then will be complete, and all will be at rest.
Joy unbounded forever reigns, laude and honor at it's best.

The Lord be glorified in praise, with unbounded love forever.
All who live victors will be, through faith and it's endeavor.

Revelation has much more to tell, study this book to learn,
Please don't wait till it's to late, God's love you should not spurn.

It's offered free, won't you accept, the victory will be sweet.
Grander than man's imagination. Lay your heart at Jesus' feet.

...So then, men ought to regard us as servants of Christ and as those entrusted with the secret things of God. Now it is required that those who have been given a trust must prove faithful...I Corinthians 4: 1, 2...NIV...If you have any encouragement from being united with Christ, if any comfort from His love, if any fellowship with the Spirit, if any tenderness and compassion, then make my joy complete by being like-minded, having the same love, being one in spirit and purpose. Do nothing out of selfish ambition or vain conceit, but in humility consider others better than yourselves. Each of you should look not only to your own interest, but also to the interest of others. Your attitude should be the same as that of Christ Jesus:...Philippians 2: 1-5...NIV

A Trust To Keep Have I

I was not born within a stable, a babe of greatest worth.
I would not bear upon my shoulders, the sins of all the earth.
Although I can be gentle and loving to the lost,
I carry not upon my back, the stripes that carry cost.

I cannot heal a sickness, or stop the sway of grief.
I can't tear down the walls of hate, in which some place belief.
Miracles, I cannot do, but as long as I shall live,
putting faith in Jesus Christ, I'll share what I can give.

In learning of the sacrifice that Jesus made for me,
and of the heavy price He paid, I knew I could be free.
Now there are so many things that I can do each day,
maybe not of miracles, but just helping on my way.

I can give freely of my love, as Jesus gave to me.
I can soothe some wounded soul whose pain my eyes can see.
I can give the gift of laughter ringing in the air,
and I can let the lonely know, there is someone to care.

I can lend a helping hand, even when I have no purse.
I can lift a broken spirit that may feel it has been cursed.
I can listen to one's suffering and hold their hearts so near.
I can give a ray of sunshine's light to dry away their tears.

I can offer Jesus, and His teachings that are strong.
Through His love I offer them a way to ease the wrong.
No I can't offer miracles, but a trust to keep have I.
In my countenance may all see from wherein His love lies.

Jesus taught me by His example, to serve, not to receive,
to love my neighbors as my friends, tell them why I believe.
I cannot change a world gone dark, but I can share His Light
that brings sweet peace into my soul, and makes my joy so bright.

Thank you Jesus, for Your love, that glows within my heart.
A trust You gave to each of us, may I always do my part.
Your love to me was given free, Lord may I do the same.
To all the others that I meet, may I do it in Your name.

A trust to keep have I dear Lord, as do others who believe.
Thank You for the life You give, the love we all receive.
Just as You pass Your love to me, I pass it on to them.
Everyday, long as I live, till face to face I meet with Him.

In Christ we are one spirit, Your trust is ours to keep.
There is no measure that's too great, when love is what we reap.
By word of mouth, by deed of hand, by giving what each can,
this trust You gave to each of us, we'll share with all of man.

...My help comes from the Lord, the Maker of heaven and earth. He will not let your foot slip – He who watches over you will not slumber:...The Lord will keep you from all harm – He will watch over your life: the Lord will watch over your coming and going, both now and forevermore...Psalm 121: 2, 3 , 7, & 8...KJV Let the morning bring me word of your unfailing love, for I have put my trust in you... Psalm 143: 8 KJV The Lord is gracious and compassionate, slow to anger and rich in love. The Lord is good to all; He has compassion on all He has made. Your Kingdom is an everlasting kingdom, and your dominion endures through all generations. The Lord is faithful to all His promises and loving toward all He has made. The Lord upholds all those who fall and lifts up all who are bowed down...The Lord watches over all who love Him...Psalm 145: 8, 9, 13, 14, 17, 18, & 20 KJV...

My Father's Love

My Father is a guiding light whose love has shown the way.
A beacon in my darkest hours when temptation leads astray.
He often sends down courage when fear would make me quiver.
His love's a glow that warms me when the cold world makes me shiver.

My Father is a source of strength whenever mine grows weak.
His power over trials of life above the thunder speaks.
He's eased my hurts and dried my tears; given hope when it was needed.
He stands beside me even when His words I have not heeded.

My Father has believed in me, in all that I can be.
Every day, long as I live, I know He's loving me.
He thinks I am more special that the riches of the earth.
He's given more of love to me than I am ever worth.

Yet I hope He sees through me, the reflection of His glow
is now a beacon shining bright for my children as they grow.
My Father's passed His love to me, I'll do the same for them.
I'll give of all He gave to me, just as I learned from Him.

And others too, I'll tell the same, for as long as I shall live.
How they are stronger with His love, and all He has to give.
He is the Alpha, and Omega, the beginning and the end.
He is my rock, my shelter, my comfort and my friend.

His love is an eternal flame, that stands the test of time,
long as it's passed from heart to heart, as it was passed to mine.
Generations come and go, but His love stands steadfast.
No amount of time can dim the glow His love has cast.

...”For I was hungered, and ye gave Me meat: I was thirsty, and ye gave Me drink: I was a stranger, and ye took Me in: Naked, and ye clothed Me: I was sick and ye visited Me: I was in prison and ye came unto Me:” Then shall the righteous answer Him, saying, "Lord, when saw we Thee an hungered, and fed Thee? Or thirsty, and gave Thee drink? When saw we Thee a stranger, and took Thee in? or naked, and clothed Thee? Or when saw we Thee sick, or in prison, and came unto Thee? And the King shall answer and say unto them, "Verily I say unto you, Insomuch as ye have done it unto one of the lest of these My brethren, ye have done it unto me...Matthew 25: 35 – 40 KJV

In The Circle Of Jesus' Love

In the circle of Jesus' love, there is a place for all.
We are no more, we are no less, than others Christ did call.
When we come to Paradise, all souls will be entwined.
But here below, we walk alone, our destinies to find.

Some find within the path they walk, people with love to share.
While others seem so lonely, there's no one who seems to care.
Some lives are filled with bounty, given much more than they need.
Some share with others what they have, some only show their greed.

Some may have warmth and comfort, some no place to lay their head.
Some seem to have no cares at all, while some know only dread.
Me, I have my ups and downs, just as all people do.
The one thing I have learned the most, this message here so true.

The pain that I or others feel, in body or in soul,
will never be appeased if hearts are shut up, dark, or cold.
Some people stay too busy, to see the pain that's borne,
to feel the weighted heartbreak of dreams trampled and torn.

It is not their intention to be heartless, to be cold.
It's just that they're too busy with their own desires so bold.
They do not stop to realize that what they throw away,
could ease the ache of someone who has had no hope to sway.

Some people will go knocking, who want to do their share;
how sad so many turn away, they haven't time to care.
It all seems so mundane to them, just another beggar's plea.
Yet just the smallest gesture does so much for one in need.

Didn't Jesus teach us His golden rule we should obey?
To do to others as ourselves is walking in Christ's way?
We are no more, we are no less than those we see each day.
Cannot the heart be opened up to one who knows dismay?

Young or old, it matters not, 'tis the love that glows within
can warm and feed the darkest gloom to let the sunshine in.
For in the circle of Jesus' love, there is a place for all.
Where each one individually feels love on their spirit fall.

Someday we'll reach that Paradise where love will be entwined.
Lord lead the path of those so lost, help them one friend to find.
Touch the heart of those with more, that they may understand.
May reach out with a gesture sweet, to lend a helping hand.

Then love will flow down here below, as freely as above.
All then will know a better place, where dreams can bloom with love.
In the circle of Jesus' love, there is a place for all.
We are no more, we are no less, on kindness may we call.

If we have no purse to give, love flows free from our hearts.
Perhaps love might be just the thing for healing there to start.
Time is too short, but living with no love at all to give,
can leave a sharp and bitter taste to those who that way live.

In the circle of Jesus' love, in warmth and solace we can bask.
We'll find the joys of giving are much more that we could ask.
I love so much that circle, it warms my heart to see,
That others too, believe as I. Forever may this be.

...Come unto Me, all ye that labour and are heavy laden, and I will give you rest. Take My yoke upon you, and learn of Me; for I am meek and lowly in heart: and ye shall find rest unto your souls. For My yoke is easy, and My burden is light...
  Matthew 11: 28 –30 KJV

Why Won't You Come?

My house of prayer was built for you, why do you sit so still?
Can't you feel Me tugging, hoping that My love you feel?
"Others are watching," you may say. They have not what you need.
The dreams you have, I can fulfill, why won't you come to Me?

You came here with a hunger, but you still will not be fed.
You're lost, or hurt or angry, and yet you won't be led.
Don't you know My love's so great, I sent My Son to die
that your salvation be complete; what more child must I try?

Why not let Christ be you light, for it grieves me that you falter.
Come let me set your world aright, lay your burdens on my alter.
Why won't you come and rest in Me, I'm waiting for your call.
I'll shelter you beneath My wings, I'll never let you fall.

Kneel at My alter in your heart, let Christ become your King.
Don't linger by the wayside, for you I can do great things.
Only My love is this true, but you must come to Me and ask.
I will stand firm in your stead, come forth to My love bask.

Why won't you come and seek My heart, for I am you Creator.
Please don't brush Me to the side, or wait to seek me later.
Though I am always waiting with patience and with grace,
the time may come too soon for you, eternity to face.

Why won't you come right now and let Me be the life you choose,
before the time has passed too swift, before you really lose?
Don't sit there waiting, wondering, if My promises are true!
Why won't you come, accept on faith as I have faith in you?

Why let your heart keep searching, I'm right here for you to find.
Just come now to My alter, and let Me ease your mind.
Soak up all that I have planned, that's waiting just for you.
Let Me be your loving guide, steadfast, constant, and true.

Why won't you come, I'm calling, come now, My love receive!
Please don't sit there empty, please don't turn away and leave!
Come seek My Son's salvation, your price's already paid.
For on the cross of Calvary, My Son's precious life was laid.

He rose victorious from the grave, your heart to live within.
Hear Him knocking at it's door? Come turn away from sin.
As He lives so then shall you, if you will just believe.
Come now! Kneel before Me, humbly ask and you'll receive.

Salvation and forgiveness for all eternity is yours.
Listen as I beckon you, to open wide the doors.
My joy will fill you fully, through all trials, pain or strife.
My grace will be sufficient for every need you have in life.

Please, come now to My alter, let Jesus be your rock.
Don't let fear or apathy into your heart be locked.
My love is for the taking, I so much long for yours.
Why won't you let Me show you all the love I hold in store?

Are you too proud to offer your heart, you life to Me?
Do you think I'll turn away? NO! That would never be!
Why won't you come and seek me, I'm so easy to be found.
Why won't you let me show you how much My love is bound.

I've waited your whole lifetime, you could come if you just would.
Why won't you let Me love you as no other ever could?
I'm still waiting, precious child, for you to heed My call.
Why won't you come and rest in Me, I'll be your all in all.

...Even the sparrow has found a home, and the swallow a nest for herself, where she may have her young – a place near Your alter, O Lord Almighty, my King and my God. Blessed are those who dwell in Your house; they are ever praising You. Blessed are those whose strength is in You, who have set their hearts on pilgrimage. Blessed is the man whose strength is in Thee; in whose heart are the ways of them...They go from strength to strength, till each appears before God in Zion... Better is one day in Your courts than a thousand elsewhere;...For the Lord God is a sun and shield, the Lord bestows favor and honor; no good thing does He withhold from those whose walk is blameless. O Lord Almighty, blessed is the man who trusts in You...
   Psalm 84: 3- 5, 7, 10 – 12 NIV

The Family of God

For each one of us there are times when Satan's fury is unfurled.
Times of tribulation when we just can't face the world.
Our lives seem to be shattered, with broken pieces all around.
When the joys of life seem distant and no comfort can be found.

When you are in the family of our most precious Lord,
there is comfort all around us non-believers can't afford.
When you are in God's family, you not only can receive,
you're in a place where you can help, encourage and relieve.

And that is what believers do, lift one another up,
anytime we feel there's too much sorrow in our cup.
Tragedy and heartbreak we alone can't overcome.
Remember you are loved so much, God sacrificed His Son.

He knows how much our heart breaks, but through His saving grace,
we have a family that's worldwide, to understand our place.
Sometimes we may feel others cannot truly understand,
unless they shared what you have lived, but faith does help us stand.

Though our hearts may be broken, in the family of our Lord,
we know we'll see a better day, if in Him our heartbreak's stored.

He's reaching to you daily, why won't you let Him in?
Why won't you trust in Jesus as your Savior and your friend?

He'll send the comfort that we need, though grace, family and friends.
Because He loves us all so much, His joys can't truly end.
Take heart that all around you, love is there just for the taking.
Do not stand upon you own, if your heart is still breaking.

Those who love our Father, His Spirit and His Son,
are much more blessed than those that don't whenever life is done.
To face life's trials so many times makes each one feel alone.
Remember that our Lord is always there to make us strong.

We can't rely on our own strength, but in numbers, strength can be
much stronger than if left alone, reach out to His family.
Remember to be thankful for the family of our Lord.
For all the love and care received, for each touch of support.

God's love is always with us, given freely from each heart
Just call upon His precious name, His love to help impart.
How blessed it is that we may be in His heart evermore.
His family is a mighty fortress, all stand in one accord.

Their wondrous love can conquer when our own hearts seem so weak.
In lifting one another up, His love above all storms can speak.
With grateful hearts, whatever grief our lives will have to meet,
we're blessed to have God's family near, their comfort we can seek.

Don't be afraid to ask for grace, or carry burdens all alone.
The Father and His family will stand by, till once more you are strong.
There will come a time you'll get a chance to give back love.
Please don't forget God gave it first by sending Jesus from above.

With our Savior standing just within our hearts own door,
His love can change the universe, and give us hope restored.
Once we reach eternity, His family will be made complete.
We'll sing His praise forever, as we all gather at His feet.

...Ask and it shall be given you; seek, and you shall find; knock and it shall be opened into you. For everyone that asketh, receiveth; and he that seeketh findeth; and to him that knocketh it shall be opened... Matthew 7: 7 & 8 KJV

A Prayer of Need

Lord, I need a rock to cling to, I am battered, beaten, worn;
my spirit's heavy laden, my heart is being torn.
I've tried to be my bravest, but Father, I'm sinking fast.
I doubt I have the courage to hang in there and last.

At times, I feel so weary, with no place left to turn.
Each path I seem to choose Lord only brings me more concern.
Although I fight the battles with all I have to give,
each skirmish takes it's toll on me, life seems too tough to live.

I need more strength and courage than I alone can find.
Though some try, it's not enough for my inner peace of mind.
I know, Lord, there are others so much wearier than I.
I try to not be selfish, but Father, please, hear too my cry!

I need your grace to lean on, until I can be strong again.
To guide my fumbling footsteps, until once more I can stand.
Please, Father, hear my pleading, turn not away from me.
Send me Your strength and courage, that I might rest in Thee.

I'm trusting in Your promise, Your grace's sufficient for all needs.
I'm trusting your sweet Spirit will come to aid me with great speed.
Before I close this prayer of need, I thank You for Your grace.
I thank You Lord that never will You turn from me Thy face.

I believe Your love is true, and faithful without end.
I thank you Father, that with all, Your ear You sweetly lend.
I give praise to Thee, my God, as I close my prayer of need.
Trusting in Thy sufficient grace, all glory be Thy creed.

In Jesus' name,
Amen

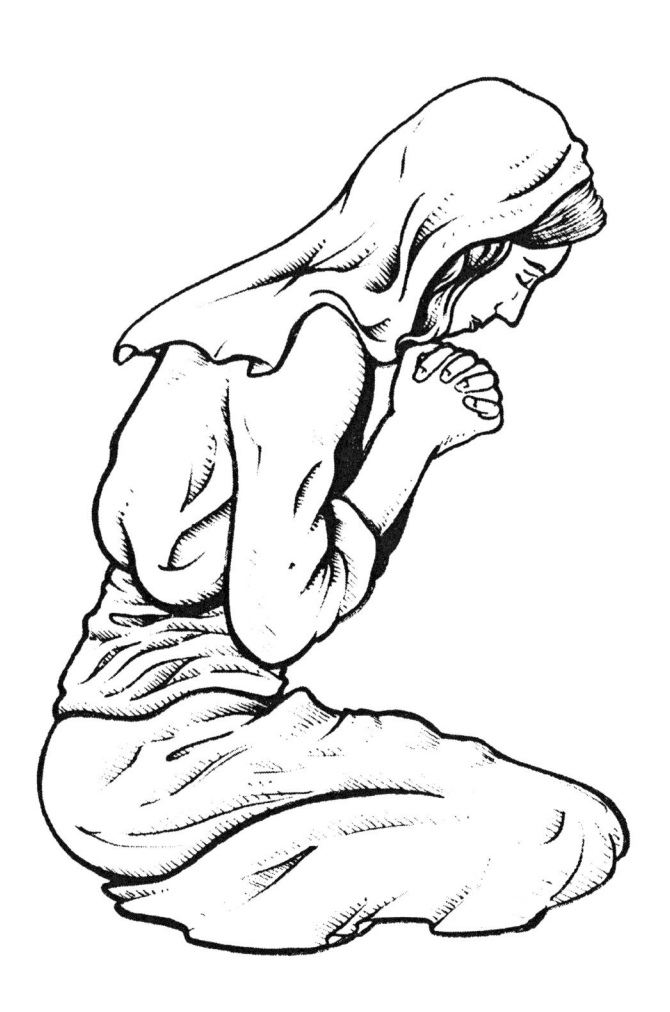

...And whatsoever ye shall ask in My name, that will I do, that the Father may be glorified in he Son. If ye shall ask any thing in My name, I will do it...And I will pray the Father, and He shall give you another Comforter, that He may abide with you forever;

...I will not leave you comfortless; I will come to you...John 14: 13, 14, 16, & 18 KJV

God's Answer To A Prayer of Need

My child, I hear your pleading. My heart's to you not cold.
Believe Me when I answer, you strength is now tenfold!
For I would never let you have more grief than you could bear.
Because I am always with you, to comfort and to share.

My grace will be sufficient, for all of your life's needs.
Did I not sacrifice My Son that you're forgiven sinful deeds?
You may not always feel My presence, but it's just a call away.
You may even doubt My answers, or fail to understand My way.

For I have plans for you to prosper, to strengthen and to grow.
I know complete fulfillment of each pathway you must know.
Remember it is darkest, before the glow of dawn.
You need not painfully be grieved to bear your pain alone.

I am the Rock you're seeking, on Me you can rely!
My courage will not falter, My strength will never die!
It's there just for the taking, you have only to believe.
Child I will not forsake you, and My love will never leave.

Though you may think I am not listening, when troubles settle in,
just trust I know what's best for you around all of life's bends.
Believe in what I promise, when needed I will help you mend.
All lives must face much sorrow, but joy comes back where it has been.

There is no tribulation that is stronger than we two,
believe in Me, as I in you. Let My love see you through.
Bless you now, My precious child, with My love everlasting!
Strength and courage I send to you, feel the hope now casting?

Have faith dear one, I love you so, forever I will be
Always steady by thy side, to fulfill every need.
I'm so glad you came to me, with all your hopes and dreams.
To bless you richly precious child, has always been my scheme.

With much love I come to you.

-God

...But this is how God fulfilled what He had foretold that through all the prohets, saying that His Christ would suffer. Repent then and turn to God, so that your sins may be wiped out, that times of refreshing may come from the Lord, and that He may send the Christ, who has been appointed for you – even Jesus. He must remain in heaven until the time comes for God to restore everything as He promised long ago through His holy prophets....Acts 3: 18 - 21 NIV...No, this is what was spoken by the prophet Joel: In the last days, God says, I will pour out My Spirit on all people. Your sons and daughters will prophesy, your young men will see visions, your old men will dream dreams....I will show wonders in the heaven above and signs on the earth below, blood and fire and billows of smoke. The sun will be turned to darkness and the moon to blood before the coming of the great and glorious day of the Lord. And everyone who calls on the name of the Lord will be saved...Acts 2: 16, 17, 19 – 21 NIV

How Many Times Must Ye Be Told?

Jesus Christ had much to do in His ministry of three years.
Crowds came to see, to be healed, to have calmed all their fears.
So many miracles He performed, no book could tell of all.
Yet of the lessons needed for us, He obeyed His Father's call.

Which think ye most important, healings or lessons taught?
Though each may last one lifetime, which one most needs to be caught?
One life, or generations, is time so urgent to be claimed?
It can be if time's borders have eternity to proclaim.

Each one has it's purpose, healings and lessons learned.
Each one Jesus used because His love so passionately burned.
It broke His heart that suffering had come into this world.
That's not how life was meant to be; till sin became unfurled

He only had three years to heal, He healed all those who came.
He only had three years His Father's message to proclaim.
Who would not accept a miracle, if it was offered free.
His teachings too would bear no price, yet they each man will need.

If God's word is studied, it's clear to see what's best for us.
Why does man reject His life, why not seek, learn and discuss?
So much more is given in God's word than just a book.
So much more can be reaped, if one will take the time to look.

The Old Testament lays the groundwork for much we need to know.
The New Testament bears the good news, that Jesus came to show.
Too many miracles to be listed, but each given had a cause.
The lessons so much needed, they should cause the heart to pause.

Take the time to look much deeper, we all could learn so much
Reconsider, look and see, let His word your heart touch.
Search how many times He healed, the blind who'd never seen.
How many times he cast out evil spirits that were unclean.

How many who could not stand or walk, yet did at His command.
How many could not speak or hear, until lives crossed with this man.
How many lay on deathbeds, yet He made them well again.
How many died, or lay entombed then rose, be it child or man.

How many times He reached out, healed lepers, so despised.
How many times He told us of the ways sin is disguised.
How many times He fed the hungry who gathered 'round in throngs.
How many parables that He taught, each with a message strong.

How many times He warned us to stand firm on faith alone.
How many time He begged us let Him our sins atone.
How many lessons He gave on faith, on what we should believe
How many times He told the only way God's love can be received.

How many times He taught of love, compassion and mercy given.
How many times He said, "Repent," and ye shall be forgiven."
Three years Jesus gave to man His heart, His soul, His love.
Three short years of obedience to His beloved Father up above.

Three years, just a blink of time, yet look at all His life has meant.
Down throughout the centuries, see just how one life was spent?
"Father, please forgive them, for they know not what they do."
Even in His dying, He left us with this message true:

The Father loves the Son, just as the Son loves true His Father.
But even greater for mankind, a love that carries even farther.
How many times must we be told, before we dare believe?
How much more could one life give, God's victory to receive?

His life for us, our life from Him, great will be our rewards,
As long as we are willing, to accept His truth, His sword.
Now is the time that you should choose to heed the Master's call.
At judgment day, too late, will be the chance to reap it all.

How many times must He reach out, He grace to be received?
How many times do you have left, before you will believe?
Please don't wait, I beg of you, He's pressed it on my heart.
To tell as many as I could, may I do faithfully my part.

If you already seek Him, give Him honor, glory, praise.
Then all hearts will be united, as our joy in Him is raised!
If I tell all, and you tell all, as do others who believe,
Our Savior's life was worth the cost, the agony received.

How many times must man be told? As long as we shall breathe!
Repeat it all! Time and again! His message to unsheathe.
Its worth is so far greater than any other to be found.
As forever in His love with grace we will all abound.

...The Spirit and the Bride say, "Come!" And let him who hears say, "Come!" Whoever is thirsty, let him come; and whoever wishes, let him take the free gift of the water of life...Revelation 22: 17 NIV

Christ, The Greatest Miracle Of All

The miracles of Christ are of greatest renown.
They have lasted from the earliest centuries on down.
Do you believe He still performs some miracles today.
I believe He does, in many very different ways.

His miracles of old, till the end of time are told.
Have you heard lately of any new ones to behold?
As Jesus lives, yes even now, within believer's faithful hearts,
He still moves mountains, still offers life with each new day He starts.

Listen with your heart, and soon you too will hear
How Jesus is still touching lives, still holds man-kind so near.
How often does the news we hear or see give glad reports
Of wondrous, miraculous events, of all kinds, of all sorts.

How lives are saved from tragedy, how sick are being healed.
Stop! Listen! Many tell of miracles that they have seen be spilled.
Science can't explain all how a miracle now takes place.
Only God could keep up with such a force of mighty pace.

Disaster may strike anyone, devastations may occur.
Tragedy may knock one down, bloody wars may still be spurred.
Yet through each battle we may find, that it always seems
To be great warriors victorious, among those broken dreams.

A life that has been saved, when only seconds just before,
It faced the darkest fear of all, death standing at its door.
Any moment life may be taken by some unexpected, quick events,
by accident, or illness, by hatred's careless or greedy intents.

Even when these things may happen, how often is there heard
Inspiration being gained by something by the deed or word.

Physically, we may doubt that Christ is seen so near.
But He's behind the scenes to offer each His heart right here.

We may not His breath on us , we can not touch His gown,
but we can call for His mighty powers to bring miracles on down.
He may not always answer us, the way we think He surely must,
But answer us He always does, our part is just to trust.

We only see a small part of God's plans for each and all,
While He sees the whole picture, how He means for things to fall.
Our Father knows what best, it not just one that He sees.
For all the earth has His best will, His heart the best of ease.

Yes, I believe in miracles; and the greatest is our Christ!
Won't you come believe with me, accept His sacrifice.
His love is always faithful, always standing ever true.
His love is will not be bound, it is a special love for you.

What can be the measure of one eternal and true friend?
Can't you see there is no measure, when love lies so rich within?
Yes, I believe in miracles, I see so many every day.
May you come and believe with me, this I must often pray.

Faith will help you see so many of His miracles galore.
Call out today to Jesus Christ, your Savior, your Lord.
I promise He won't fail you, God's promises the same.
He never fails in His promises, place trust in His sweet name.

Thank you dear Father, from my heart, for the miracles You've given.
For the greatest miracle of all: Christ who came to bring us home to heaven.
Lift high all ye nations, let every voice with praise ring true!
For the Father, for the Son, for their most Holy Spirit too.

Three entities all stand as one, three different yet the same.
All praise, honor and glory needs be raised in sweet Jehovah's name.
Yes, I believe in all of His miracles, and long as I live, I will.
No greater joy will ere be known than with His love being filled.

Would you like to see your manuscript become a book?

If you are interested in becoming a PublishAmerica author, please submit your manuscript for possible publication to us at:

acquisitions@publishamerica.com

You may also mail in your manuscript to:

**PublishAmerica
PO Box 151
Frederick, MD 21705**

We also offer free graphics for Children's Picture Books!

www.publishamerica.com

PublishAmerica